Growing a Runner

Growing a Runner

GERRY GARCIA

Copyright © 2017 Gerry Garcia

All rights reserved. No part of this publication may be reproduced, distributed or transmitted in any form or by any means, including photocopying, recording, or other electronic or mechanical methods, without the prior written permission of the publisher, except in the case of brief quotations embodied in critical reviews and certain other noncommercial uses permitted by copyright law.

ISBN# 978-0-692-93985-7

DEDICATION

This book is dedicated to Cipriano D. "Cip" Esquibel, in memoriam

Cipriano was my supervisor for the University of New Mexico, Educational Administration Preparation Program in 1993. I learned a lot from him. He would always introduce me as, "Gerry and I go way back." Cip was a wrestling coach at Rio Grande High School in Albuquerque, New Mexico, when I was running cross-country for El Rito Normal School.

He was the Albuquerque Public Schools personnel director for 24 years. After retiring in 1994, he was director of the City's Human Resource Department. He was respected and admired and loved by many who knew him.

Cipriano was born near Wagon Mount, New Mexico, a small town, 165 miles from Albuquerque and was raised in Rock Ford, Colorado.

He was a champion prep wrestler and distance runner in high school at Rocky Ford where he graduated in 1951.

In 1957, Cipriano started coaching and teaching at Rio Grande High School. He racked up an incredible record of 12 individual state champions, eight runner-up, and had two Rio Grande teams that took runner-up honors in State High School Wrestling Tournament.

CONTENTS

Preface ◉ i

Acknowledgments ◉ v

Introduction ◉ vii

Chapter 1:
Find A Passion and Running With It ◉ 1

Chapter 2:
My First High School Race ◉ 25

Chapter 3:
Training On Forest Road 44 ◉ 43

Chapter 4:
High School, Eighth Grade State
Cross-Country Champion ◉ 63

Chapter 5:
Five Straight High School Championships ◉ 83

About The Author ◉ 101

PREFACE

I've known success; I wouldn't be writing this book if I hadn't. I was the star of my high school team, and won five consecutive state cross-country championships — a remarkable achievement, to be sure, and, reading this, you might remember that old phrase, "winning is everything." But consider this: I've known defeat as well. I've lost many races. I qualified for the Olympic trials three times, and never made the team. The reality is, not everyone is going to win a trophy and not everyone is going to make the team. So why do we compete? The reason is passion. Every time you fall short in achieving your goal, you fall back on your reserve of passion. It is your safety net. Passion will push you through difficult times and drive you to get better, no matter what.

Throughout the book, the word "passion" will pop up, so let's be clear on its meaning. Robert Vallerand, president of the International Positive Psychology

Association, defined passion as: "a strong inclination towards a self-defining activity that people love, that they consider important, and to which they devote a significant amount of time and energy." Here's an example: My daughter, Clarissa, loves to read. When she gets passionate about something, she'll read about it and research it for countless hours. Her passions don't strike her fully formed. They take work — research, study — to develop. Passion doesn't just happen to you overnight. Your biggest passion might have surfaced early in life. Sometimes you might not even recognize it as a passion, thinking of it only as an interest or obsession. When I was in second grade, I read a story about a boy who won races by using his long legs, and it inspired me to run. I became obsessed. I ran everywhere. I preferred to run instead of walk. I even got in trouble in class for running to the pencil sharpener. As punishment, I had to run for fifteen minutes around the playground. Little did the substitute teacher know, it was a punishment I enjoyed! The next day, when my teacher returned to school, she gave me a kickball to keep me occupied during recess. I'd run and kick it and the other boys and girls would chase it madly. I just thought running was fun, but my teacher realized I was developing a passion, and she gave me the opportunity to pursue it.

In the introduction to my book I discuss the things I have in common with elite runners in the Rift Valley in Kenya, runners renowned world-wide for their dominance in long-distance races. Our upbringings were similar, but more interesting than that is the passions we both developed in our early years. We're drawn together not by how we were raised, but by the passions we raised and nurtured in ourselves: a passion for running, a desire to race, and the knowledge that winning isn't everything. What matters is passion.

With coach Ruben O. Lucero, Sr: L-R: Rudy Jaramillo, Pressy Archuleta, Chris Martinez, Billy Trujillo and me.

ACKNOWLEDGMENTS

The story that I bring you is true. Many of the characters in this story who were important in my life are no longer with us. While writing this book, I struggled with my emotions and had to put down my pen and paper when recalling experiences with these people. I am thankful that our paths crossed.

Rafelita Chavez, Alberto Fernandez, Martha Guardolia, Marie Hansen, Gimma Hermina, Mary Kulnane, Ponciano Madrill (El Rito), and Olivia Garcia-Ortiz, thank you for your cheers and encouragement.

Thanks to Deborah Pedue at Illumination Graphics for turning the manuscript into a wonderful design of the book.

Tara Thelen at Illumination Graphics' artwork helped to produce a beautiful book cover design.

Special thanks to William Bostwick and Michael Burwell for editing my book on such a short notice and fixing everything that needed to be corrected.

A big hug to my daughter, Clarissa, an aspiring writer who motivated me to take the plunge and write this book. I love you.

And finally, "With God all things are possible" (Matthew 19:26).

INTRODUCTION

Gerry Garcia and the Rift Valley Runners

Gerry Garcia was born and raised in El Rito, New Mexico. He won the New Mexico state high school cross-country championship five years in a row, from 1961 to 1965, a state record. (He might have won six, had he been eligible, but seventh graders were not allowed to compete in the state high school championships.) In five years, Gerry lost only two cross-country races. What is even more extraordinary is that for 50 years, no other runner in New Mexico has achieved quite a feat.

In recent years there has been significant interest in the factors that contributed to his success, in his humble upbringing and fierce determination in the face of obstacles. Gerry's story is special, but it is not unique. Winning five titles is a reachable goal for anyone who dares to achieve it. In fact, Gerry's remarkable success has parallels halfway around the world to the Rift Valley in Kenya, a country that produces the world's best distance runners.

Gerry grew up running in a similar terrain, living in an agricultural rural environment, and having a similar diet. El Rito and Kenya's Rift Valley have similar terrain: rolling hills and flat stretches, picturesque fields and pastures. The elevation of the Rift Valley is approximately 7,000 feet. El Rito is at 6,875 feet, but Gerry trained in an area in El Rito that is between 7,400 and 7,950 feet. The weather in both places is conducive for training, with the right balance between temperature and humidity. In El Rito, the hottest day of the year is around 86 degrees. The January low is 17. In the Rift Valley, the highs are in the 80s, and the lows in the 50s. Both El Rito and the Rift Valley get equal amount of rain — actually a good thing for running. Rain can keep runners from overheating and makes running more comfortable.

Agriculture plays a big role in both economies. Gerry came from a poor rural family who lived on welfare because both of his parents were disabled. Rift Valley runners come from poor rural families, too. Money is not the primary motivation for running for runners that live in Rift Valley, but can offer a way out of poverty to a very select few. The same was true for Gerry. His parents could not afford to pay for his education, but success in high school earned him a full scholarship to Eastern New Mexico University and Lamar University. Rift Valley children are seen running back and forth from school — the passion for running starts early there. Gerry too ran to school with his brothers from elementary school through high school, a two mile round trip.

Gerry's diet was similar to that of Rift Valley runners, a contributing factor to their successes. They eat high-carbohydrate food and proteins, like potatoes, beans, bread, and vegetables. Meat or milk is not a standard item of their diet. Neither is alcohol. Gerry grew up eating beans and potatoes with whole wheat tortillas for lunch and supper, and hot cakes and syrup or oatmeal with powdered milk for breakfast. Dessert was not a regular part of his meals, but they had baked apples from fresh apples that were donated to his family by a local farmer in the community. To drink, water or powdered milk. Spinach was common in the spring, picked fresh in the alfalfa fields near his house. Meat was not his main source of protein. Gerry's father would buy an old sheep for $5.00 when sheepherders in El Rito were selling. There were no seconds and no snacking between meals.

Genetics might have played a role in Gerry's success, but studies disagree on the relative importance of inherited traits versus culture. If Gerry inherited genes from his parents to excel in running, they were probably his skinny arms and legs. Still, dozens of studies have confirmed that factors such as reflex capabilities, metabolic efficiency, and lung capacity are evenly distributed among the human population. What differs is culture.

Rift Valley parents encourage their children to stay physically active at an early age by having them walk or run to school and work in the fields. Gerry's father hired someone to drive his children to and from school mornings, but stopped when the driver proved unreliable, and Gerry started to run.

While there are many similarities between Gerry and Rift Valley runners, there is one difference. While children in the Rift Valley can look to elite runners who have grown wealthy with their earnings from international racing, Gerry had no role model runners as a child. Indeed, even to see someone walking briskly for exercise in his home town was irregular. Role models for a child aspiring to become a distance runner were simply not there. Gerry's dad and mom were not parents on the sidelines, shouting and cheering, and hoping that their child would get good enough to win an athletic scholarship. Gerry's parents were disabled and never got to see Gerry run. His dad was

INTRODUCTION

nearly blind and his mother was mentally ill. However, Gerry became a town treasure, with a crew of devoted fans that followed him to all his cross country and track meets. He wasn't born into a supportive culture, but he created one around his talents.

Gerry's is a story of just that kind of solitary determination and self-made success. Gerry's achievements are his own, grown from humble soil with sweat and determination. If he can do it — if Kenyan runners can do it — so can you.

By **Clarissa O. Garcia**

CHAPTER 1:

Finding A Passion and Running With It

Born To Run

I was the third of eight children, born and raised in El Rito, a little village in the wilds of northern New Mexico. My parents, Pedro and Octaviana Garcia, learned a hardscrabble life, growing up poor during the Great Depression, and instilled those values in me.

My mother helped her parents, Geronimo and Adela Martinez, on their small subsistence farm. They raised sheep, cows, and other animals, and grew vegetables and fruit in gardens and orchards. They gathered pinon nuts from local forests. In good years, my mother could fill a 100-pound sack in one day. They bought a few things at the general store, but mostly ate what came off their land, or what they could barter for from the neighbors. Families looked after each other during that time.

My father's dad and mother were farmers too, and also devoted Catholics. When my father was in his late 40s, he was a member of Los Penitente, a group of men in the community who practiced penance, or repentance of their sins, including flagellation during La Semana Santa (Holy Week), symbolizing the crucifixion of Jesus Christ — a practice prohibited by the Roman Catholic Church. According to my father, each member would be subjected to flagellation in a dark room by another member wearing a hood over his face so that he would not be recognized. It was a painful, but profound rite of passage for the men, and bonded them together in their faith.

My father was 25 at the start of the Great Depression, a young man but he had already lived a long and challenging life. His mother, Jenoveva, died when he was 15, and he lived with his father, Sofio. During the Depression, my father worked on the railroad in Wyoming as a track foreman, supervising maintenance and construction crews. During World War II, he worked as a welder in

Wyoming, cutting steel in the manufacture of ships. In 1946, my father tried his hand at entrepreneurship, opening a small neighborhood bar in El Rito, but two years later, he shut it down to marry my mother. He didn't love his life wiping glasses and pouring pints, and was afraid the children he and his new bride planned to have might follow in his footsteps.

After closing his bar, my father had to work quite a distance from home because jobs were scarce. Our family missed him very much, but we knew he worked hard to support us because of how much he cared.

We lived humbly but well. I never went hungry and never saw my diet as eating poor. Lunch and dinner was usually a big pot of beans, a large pan of potatoes, fried in water, and a stack of whole wheat tortillas. Spinach was common in the spring. For desert, we ate baked apples. Breakfast on weekends was whole wheat flour hot cakes with syrup. During the week we had oatmeal with powdered milk and a glass of water or powdered milk. My mother used to make tortillas from white flower, but I convinced her to make them out of whole wheat flour when I was in the second grade after eating a tortilla made by my friend's mom. It was delicious hearty and medium-brown — the first time I had seen one that color.

Meat was not a regular item in our menu. Once a year, my father would buy an old mutton sheep for five dollars. Meat and perishables would spoil quickly because we didn't have a refrigerator or a freezer. In fact, we didn't even have electricity. It wasn't until I was in second grade that the house was wired. Drying meat was not a good preserving method because the fatty tissue quickly became rancid.

My father was 5'5" and lean, with black hair and dark skin. Only I inherited this trait from him. I remember coming home from school one afternoon when I was in first grade, grabbing a sock, soaking in water, and using it to scrub my face because my teacher told me I was getting too black from drinking coffee. "What are your doing to your face?" my father asked me. "Making myself white," I replied. "Geronimo, women like dark-skinned guys," he said. We stuck together — small but strong. The two of us were, literally, the black sheep of the family

My mother was 5'1", leaning toward lean, with black hair, green hazel eyes, and light, white skin. I have an old, curling photograph of her, taken when she was in her 30s. She's standing, looking very pretty in a flowered dress, and wearing a brimmed hat.

Neither of my parents were runners, and I don't think that I inherited any so-called "long distance" genes from them. But perhaps I should still thank them for this trait — it might be because of when I was born. Studies suggest that elite athletes born in the first three months of the year have a competitive edge over those born later in the year, in terms of cardiovascular fitness, muscle strength, and their ability to accelerate (important in competitive sports). All athletes at the Beijing Olympics were born in the first three months of the year. A 2004 study compared the births of top marathon runners from seven countries that ran sub-2:18 for men and sub-2:43 for women and found most runners on the lists were born in January. I was born in February. Who knows? Maybe it helped.

Of course, birth isn't the only factor in making a great athlete, and I can't give it all the credit for my success. But it's interesting to think about. My father and my brother, Sofio, were both born in February as well, but my father was not an athlete and Sofio was a mediocre runner in high school. Still, my father did not have the same opportunities to participate in running as I did so I have no way of knowing how good a runner he could have been.

If I inherited any genetic advantage from my parents to excel in running it was probably my body type: small and kind of skinny. I guess I inherited the best possible genetic body types combination from both parents.

Even with an auspicious birth and advantageous build, I lacked the kinds of advantages many other young athletes have. It's not like I grew up in an athletically

Gerry (4th grader) and Sofio (7th grader) with their dad

oriented environment. To see someone walking briskly for exercise in my hometown was irregular. Role models for runners — any kind of athlete, for that matter — were simply not present. There were no running clubs for children to teach me that running was fun.

My parents were supportive, but not overbearing. They never even saw me run. They weren't the stereotypical "sports" parents you see cheering at the sidelines — or, more often, arguing with the refs. My mom didn't walk around with running shoes and my dad didn't play catch with us in the backyard. In fact, both of my parents were living with serious illnesses. My dad suffered from diabetes and was nearly blind; my mother suffered from mental illness, and was in and out of mental hospitals as I was growing up. However, my father was very energetic despite suffering from diabetes. I recall going to the city with my father when I was in the second grade and having difficult staying up with his walking pace.

They might not have taught me how to ride a bike or throw a ball, but above all, my parents taught me resilience. In fact, I might have even inherited that inner strength from them. A 2006 study in Harvard Mental Health suggests a genetic disposition helps some people endure stress and bounce back. We often hear of athletes overcoming challenges to achieve their goals. Some years back, Stephen Martinez of Poqaoque High School, Poqaoque, New Mexico, won the Class 3A boys state cross-country championship with only one shoe. He lost his shoe during the race. Martinez is a good example of a "psychologically resilient" person. A reporter once asked my high school coach what he attributed to my five state cross country titles. My coach said, "He had something inside of him that no one else had." Maybe he was talking about that mysterious inner strength — the power of Superman hidden inside mild-mannered Clark Kent. Who knows what powers you have inside you, until you find a passion in which to put them on display.

Desire For Running

I didn't know that I had a passion for running, but I had a desire to run. Desire is one thing, but passion is another. Desire is simple — I wanted to move fast! — but passion is complex. Don't underestimate the power of desire; without it, I never would have developed into the runner I became. But don't equate it with true, sustaining passion. Passion does not lie dormant inside and then suddenly jumps out and grabs you. Passion is a seed you have to plant and cultivate. Like raising vegetables in your garden, it takes hard work, dedication, and investment. But when it grows, grab it and don't let go.

FINDING A PASSION AND RUNNING WITH IT

Here's an example from my own life that might help illustrate the point. My daughter Clarissa and I planted 10 small evergreens in the front yard. My daughter soon lost interest in helping me care for them because they weren't growing quickly enough. I forgot to tell my daughter that evergreens grew at different rates: some are fast-growing, others grow more slowly. Some grow slowly and then stop altogether. I didn't give up on my trees, though, investing in their growth by buying fertilizer and sprinkling it around them and watering them regularly. This took time, patience, and hard work. Much to my surprise, one tree stopped growing and eventually died. Two others were showing signs of dying so I relocated them: one to the backyard, the other closer to the main entrance to the house. The tree in the backyard died, despite the effort to save it. The other thrived, and is growing into a beautiful tree. It gets lots of compliments from people.

My experience growing evergreens holds lessons for people. Consider the similarities between gardening and going out for a sport. First, you have to have a desire, either to plant something or to get involved in a particular sport. This desire is the seed of your passion. Maybe it originates from experience — perhaps you've gardened before, or enjoyed gym class or recreational sports, and want the same kind of satisfaction again. When I first went out for cross country in seventh grade, I already had some experience running. I knew it was fun. I had the desire. On the team, I'd cultivate this desire into passion and success. Competition would force me to run faster and faster, and my level of satisfaction would grow. But that growth — turning desire into passion, and passion into joy — takes hard work and commitment. You must achieve passion before you can turn that passion into recognition and rewards. Like an apple tree grown from a seed, only once your labor of love starts to bear fruit will you feel that your hard work has paid off.

My daughter Clarissa has a passion for playing the violin but that wasn't always the case. When she was in the fifth grade, in a class for gifted children, she participated in a class project called the "night of the nobles." The students had to choose someone famous from the past, write their biography, dress up as that person and give a speech about their life in front of an assembly. I helped with her research. One day, I opened the encyclopedia and started flipping the pages. "Stop dad," said my daughter. "Who is that guy with the violin?" "Mozart" I answered. "Yeah, I want to learn about him," she said. We checked out some books from the public library and, after a few days of careful study, she transformed into the composer at the school assembly. This is how she got interested in playing the violin — this is what sparked her desire. The day after her presentation, I visited a music store and arranged for her to take lessons — to turn her desire into passion. But cultivation of her desire didn't come easily. It was a challenge to get her to practice at home. Twenty minutes a night seemed like forever for her. The following year, she transferred to a school in another part of the city that had a violin teacher. She learned to read music, played at concerts in middle school, took private lessons for two years, joined the Albuquerque Youth Symphony Orchestra, played solo at her church, played for students at the school where her mom teaches, and played solo at her high school graduation assembly. Today she has a four-inch-thick binder of sheets of music she enjoys playing. She is a truly passionate musician.

Clarissa was that evergreen that grows slower than others. Her passion took time to develop. Now, she is like the tree I moved to our front door: strong, tall, and showered in compliments. It can take time and effort to turn desire to passion, but you must persevere with faith that even slow-growing evergreens can become big, beautiful trees.

But what about the second tree — the one I couldn't save? In people too, sometimes passion simply doesn't grow. Sometimes someone will go out for a competitive sport and quit without developing a passion for it. Consider this hypothetical situation. In sixth grade Paul set a goal for himself: He'd go out for high school track and run the mile. He started training. He was devastated after placing last in his first track meet, and quit the team. We'll never know if Paul would have run the mile — he never grew passionate enough to try. He had the potential of becoming a great miler had he not quit the team. A dying tree can be rescued if the problem is identified and steps are taken to help the tree grow stronger. When a runner quits running, the same principle applies. The runner should identify the problem, and take steps to get running again. If that doesn't motivate him, he should try another sport.

Developing A Passion

When I started second grade, I read a story about a boy who won races by using his long legs, and it inspired me to run. I became obsessed — I ran everywhere. I preferred to run instead of walk. I even got in trouble in class for running to the pencil sharpener. As punishment, the substitute teacher, had me run for fifteen minutes around the playground. Little did the teacher know, it was a punishment I enjoyed! When my father heard about it, he made me chop wood every day in the evenings for a week. This, I didn't like as much. When my teacher, Mrs. Lola Valdez, returned to school, she gave me a kickball to keep me occupied during recess. I'd run and kick it and the other boys and girls and I would chase it madly. Mrs. Valdez realized that I was developing a passion for running and she gave me the opportunity to pursue it.

One day as I was chopping, my brother, Sofio, started teasing me. I flipped him one, threw down the axe, and bolted off. Sofio and I were actually the best of friends. He was only three years older than me, and easily rattled. I was laid back, but I like pushing his buttons — we'd get into it and he'd chase me.

Sofio caught up to me in the alfalfa field next to the house. Instead of running through the center of the field, I chose to run the perimeter, along the barbed wire fence that separated the field from our neighbors. With Sofio hot on my heels, we were off! I sprinted the first 50 yards and looked back — Sofio was 10 yards behind, huffing and puffing. He turned his sprint into a comfortable jog and I did the same. "I'm going to catch you, wait and see!" he yelled. Three-quarters of the way around the field, he stopped jogging and started walking. "Wait!" he shouted. "Let's be friends. You are just too fast." We hugged it out, laughing.

I entered my first competitive race that summer. The organizers of the "Dia de Santiago" celebration organized a fifty-yard dash. It was a spur-of-the-moment decision: The traditional tug-of-war contest between married and unmarried men had been cancelled when the rope mysteriously disappeared. The organizers went around looking for kids to join the race. A man came up to me and asked me if I wanted to run. "This boy is going to win," he told another man. Had he seen me run before? I didn't know, but I jumped in line anyway. I came in second. The man who had recruited me approached me at the finish. "What happened?" he asked. "Short legs."

The following summer, organizers added horse racing to the festivities. The races were held in a dusty dirt field on the outskirts of town. Two or three horses from El Rito and the surrounding towns ran in each heat. It was a hectic affair, made worse by the punishing sun and little shade. The horses were anxious and the race was plagued with false starts. Someone in the crowd would yell, "ya vienen!" ("they're off!") — and then another false start.

One summer, a horse trailer pulled up to the starting line and out came the most beautiful horse I had ever seen. Black, short, slender but not thin, with skinny but muscular legs, a slender neck, a long tail, and a glossy, neatly groomed coat. What caught my eye was the erect and elegant way he walked to the starting line: head high, eyes alert, ears pricked as if he was set for action. He tossed his head in confidence as he walked. "¡Ya vienen!" He went out fast and never looked back, kicking up dust — a true front-runner. His chest heaved up and down. His hooves pounded the ground into a blur of dirt and muscle. He ran so smoothly he looked like he was floating in air, only coming back to earth when he slowed to a trot long after blazing across the finish line. Of course, he won handily.

It might sound foolish, but I learned a lot from that horse. With a slight forward lean, my chest and head up, eyes forward, and never a glance behind me, arms pumping and feet light, I ran like that majestic horse. I became a champion.

At the beginning of third grade, my mother became mentally ill. My father quit his job to care for me and my siblings. When my father's diabetes became life-threatening, we went on welfare. A welfare check of $300 dollars a month (in those days food stamps were not issued) for a family of nine was not much, and we had to scrimp and save whatever extra cash we had to pay for other necessities.

There was a long history of mental illness on my mom's side of the family, and she was in and out of the hospital for the rest of her life. When my mother was not institutionalized, and could stay at home, she was good about taking her medicine. Those days, she was lovely. But when she was not on her meds, she was in her own world, speaking only to herself and the voices in her head. I rarely brought friends over. One day a boy stopped by unexpectedly to visit. The boy and I were playing when my mother walked by, talking to herself. "What is wrong with your mom?" he asked. I didn't reply. "Is she crazy?" "No," I replied. "She is ill." What bothered me was not the question, so much as the attitude he had displayed toward people with mental health problems — "mad," "crazy," "nuts." That stigma was very real in rural communities in those days. The boy never came to visit me again.

It was hard to keep my mother's condition private, but even so, there were good things about living in a small town. The African proverb that it takes a village to educate a child held true. Many neighbors helped my family in those days, but one that stands out is the Martin family. Tom and Pat Martin and their mother Margaret (I called her Mrs. Martin) were very special to me growing up. Tom owned a general store across the street from my home when I was in fourth grade, and would allow me to come over on afternoons for an hour to watch "Hopalong Cassidy" on a small, black-and-white television. Pat was a rancher and brought us boxes of apples for Christmas. I would ride in his family tractor while he cut alfalfa in his field next to our house. Mrs. Martin would hire me to cut weeds around her house. She'd show up with a peanut butter sandwich and a glass of milk when it was time for me to take a break. She always ended her visit by saying, "You are a good boy."

FINDING A PASSION AND RUNNING WITH IT

During fourth grade, I started running from our house to my grandmother's (my mother's mom) every day after school to visit her, my uncle Mike, and my brother Ben. I only stayed home when the ground was covered in white after a heavy snowfall. It was customary in those days for newlyweds to allow their first child to be adopted by grandparents, and my oldest brother Ben lived with my grandmother from when he was a baby. Ben was a smart kid — he had a tinkerer's mind and was good with his hands. He did well in electronics class. In high school, Ben made a metal detector from things he found around the farm. Ben spent most of his time in town; I hardly ever saw him at my grandmother's house. When I visited, it was usually just the two of us, and I'd spend the afternoon helping out by cleaning chicken coops and doing other chores around the farm. My grandmother repaid me with a good, hearty meal. Seeing a chicken running around with its head cut off was not pleasant for a little kid like me, but it made delicious eating! After dinner, my grandmother would walk me down to the main road and wave over the first vehicle that came along to ask for a ride for me back to my house in town.

I loved to run to my grandmother's house. She was my first coach. My grandmother would wait for me to arrive at her house and she would say, "You ran slow today" or "You ran fast today." She was very accurate in her analysis of my running. There were days when I would run slow because the weather was bad or I had a blister on my foot or a stomach ache. There were also days when the weather was sunny and great for running, and I felt great. Naturally, I would run faster. It was about two miles, and didn't take me very long. She lived on Canyon Road, but I preferred to take the "scenic route" on Forest Road 44, which ran parallel to Canyon, on the other side of El Rito Creek. Forest Road was isolated, with less traffic. If a driver ever passed me, I would shout out, "How fast I am running?" They would look at their vehicle's speedometer and shout back. I would pick up the pace, hoping to increase my speed by the time another car came along.

Rivers generally crest in September in rural areas in New Mexico. El Rito was no exception. My mother grew up near the river and knew how quickly the little creek could swell into a dangerous torrent during heavy rains. Whenever fall approached, she got nervous about my daily jaunts to grandmother's. There were no bridges; the fastest way across the river was a precarious walk over a log to the other side. I did this so many times that I was used to the challenge, but my parents feared for my life. "You are in God's hands," they'd say to me, giving me bendiciones (blessings). Las bendiciones was a Spanish tradition of having a child kneel in front of his or her parents while they lifted up their hands and made the sign of a cross. This ritual was supposed to protect the child from evil. Most of the time, my parents blessed me while I was standing because I was too anxious to start running to kneel.

Crossing the river was the least of my worries. Much worse was Maldito, my grandmother's rooster. Every day, he'd lie in wait to attack. He would bow to me when I approached, putting his wings down in display, then stand erect and wait for me to make a move. Maldito was too old to cook. My grandmother tried to give him away, but nobody wanted the old guy. Trying to tame Maldito by picking him up and holding him only made Maldito more aggressive. He would fight until there was no option but to put him down and let him have his way. As soon as I would see Maldito, I would say, "damn it." One day my grandmother asked me why I was calling the rooster "damn it." I explained that "damn it" in Spanish

meant "Maldito." I hoped my grandmother would not object to the name — he definitely deserved it.

It was the same scenario every time I visited: Maldito didn't exactly roll out the red carpet for me. He would crow as we fought, and my grandmother would come out of her house to open the screen door for me. It was only a ten-yard sprint to the door, but it was too risky: I was afraid to bump into my grandmother and knock her down, so I would sprint around the house, with the little guy right on my heels, and enter the house from the opposite direction.

Roosters generally run about nine miles per hour, and I always managed to outrun the stupid beast, but each time we ran he seemed to get closer to me. What annoyed me the most was that after chasing me into the house, he would crow a lot as he strutted away, his neck feathers puffed, as if it had won the race.

One afternoon, after Maldito chased me into the house, my grandmother said, "cerca, Geronimo" — close call. A man sitting on a chair looked at me and said, "Geronimo, the great Indian chief? You run fast. Are you Indian?" Puzzled, my grandmother responded, "No — he is named after my husband."

The stranger thought I was Indian. I was dark-skinned, with black hair and high cheekbones. My grandmother and my uncle were light-skinned with blue eyes, and my grandmother's husband was also white-skinned. I was dark, like my father. That evening when I got home, I told my father about the stranger's comments. "You are Spanish and should be proud of it. Geronimo was an Apache chief. A great warrior and a great leader." he said.

FINDING A PASSION AND RUNNING WITH IT

"Are Indians good runners?" I asked my father. "They are natural runners" he said.

Some of the best runners I've known had Native American roots. In 2016, I was honored at the 41 Annual Gardenswariz Great Southwest Track & Field Classic in Albuquerque, New Mexico, and had the pleasure of meeting Anthony Armijo. Armijo broke my mile record by two seconds. He is a Native American.

The next time I visited my grandmother, Maldito was gone. My grandmother sold the troublemaker for a dollar. She told me he was taken to a city far away. It wasn't until many years later that I realized Maldito might have been used for cock fighting. He was probably pretty good. Based on how ferociously he fought me, he was likely formidable in the ring.

When I was in fifth grade, the basketball coach, Mr. Vicente Martinez, asked me to join the team. Mr. Martinez was passionate about teaching and coaching, and knowledgeable about the sport. I told him I'd like to play, "but I can't dribble that well." "We need someone quick and fast," he replied. "And I've seen you running on the playground." I was short for the average fifth grader — under five feet — but that didn't seem to matter to Mr. Martinez. He put me on defense, and I played the entire game. I guarded my opponents closely, swarming and mimicking them. If anyone dribbled too far from his body, I would slap the ball out of his hand. Sometimes my opponent would take it personally and get belligerent. But that only meant he'd get a foul. My aggressiveness on the court forced turnovers. Maybe I learned a thing or two from Maldito.

My success on the court was not due to my basketball skills, but to my cardiovascular endurance. I could keep going even when I felt tired. The ability to keep going separates winners from losers. It's classic "mind over matter." If you can ignore the fear of getting tired, you will improve your performance.

Mr. Martinez gave me self-confidence and helped me develop my passion for running. I sat up front with him when he drove the team to games. He'd tell me, "Play like Denise Branch. Position yourself between the opponent and the basket." Denise Branch was El Rito's star player when I was in 5th grade. I remember watching him hit a shot while falling backwards — nothing but net. He set a record in 1957 for the most points scored in a single game in New Mexico high school basketball.

Sixth grade was an eventful year for me. My grandmother was in her 90s then, and had moved to a residential home in the city. She was suffering from dementia. Ben was in the Navy. He didn't register for the draft, and Uncle Sam had given him an ultimatum: join the military or spend five years in prison. He picked wisely.

FINDING A PASSION AND RUNNING WITH IT

The chickens, sheep, and cows were gone. My uncle lived alone with a few horses. Sofio and I got up at four in the morning to help my brother Pete haul wood to our house from La Quemazon, a large area of the Carson National Forest that had burned down some years back.

Pete bought a 1950 Ford truck for $50 dollars — he got it cheap because it smoked, and he only made it worse by running it on used motor oil. We couldn't afford to buy a new bottle. A big white cloud of smoke would billow behind the truck for miles when he drove. One morning, a forest ranger approached us while we were cutting wood in the forest because someone had reported seeing smoke in the area. After loading the truck, I would run the four miles back to the house because it was quicker than riding in the truck. Pete had to make several stops on the way back to cool the overheated engine.

Finally, the truck broke down for good. After that, Sofio and I hauled wood with a friend in his four-wheeled horse-drawn wagon. The truck might have been slow, but the wagon was downright dangerous. One day, we had a near-death experience that brought the enterprise to a complete halt. As we were descending a hill with a heavy load of wood, the horses got spooked and stampeded, taking the wagon — wood, kids and all — with them. My friend and I jumped off, but Sofio hung on longer, and jumped just as the wagon broke free from the horses and crashed into a tree. He landed safely, with only minor bruises, but the wagon was wrecked. I ran back to town for help.

It was an eventful year, to be sure. But there was a silver lining: My uncle Mike started visiting more often, arriving on horseback or in a horse-drawn wagon, and I started spending more time with my cousins, Tito Otiz, Sofio Ortiz, Frank Ortiz Jr, and Guzman Jaramillo Jr.

CHAPTER 2:

My First High School Race

Becoming A Distance Runner

It was my first day of high school. I was a seventh-grader. I ate a quick breakfast and left the house early, hoping the school doors would be open. I had a mission to complete before classes started that day: I was in search of treasure. Specifically, I wanted to study the collection of bronze, silver and gold trophies, commemorating the school's past victories. I was in luck — the doors were open, despite the early hour, and I entered the building and walked as fast as I could to the trophy cases. The floor was shiny and newly polished, in anticipation of the soon to arrive hordes of new students, and I was careful not to slip on the fresh wax. Since its inception in 1909, El Rito Normal School — the House of the Eagles — had always been recognized for a high standard in academics and athletics. "Más que una escuela," the motto went — more than a school. I thrilled to attend, fired up and filled with joy, pride, and a sense of belonging. I knew I was home.

I was looking for the trophy that the "Dream Team" won in basketball in 1957. There were two high school divisions in those days, A and B, and tiny El Rito completed in B division. The team played Espanola High School — Espanola was in the A division — and came up short by only 2 points.

Dennis Branch played center — he was my idol when I was in the 5th grade. He had everything it took: hard work, dedication, and consistency. He was the epitome of success. I met him for the first time in the 80s. He was working at the University of New Mexico. I reminded him of the time he hit a fade-away shot. He smiled but didn't say anything. I'd never forget his humility. Branch's basketball career ended when he sprained his ankle and tore a ligament — in inoperable injury since the tear was so close to a nerve.

MY FIRST HIGH SCHOOL RACE

My next stop was the school gym. I was going to make a pit-stop at the gym to give coach Ruben Lucero a copy of my class schedule, pick up a pair of running shoes and a warm-up suit, and then hurry to my first-period class. I would see coach Lucero again during second period for P.E. I was a little nervous, but I wasn't going to let him see it. He had coached my brothers, Pete, and Sofio, they described him as an easy-going guy

I entered the gym, overwhelmed by its grandeur. This was the first time that I had seen the gym empty. It was quiet as a cathedral, and just as beautiful, the floor so clean you could eat off it. It was as though it were a picture, perfectly framed with not a flaw to be found. The head basketball coach, Vince "Marty" Martinez, kept it spick-and-span. The bleacher seats looked brand new; the ceiling as high as the stars. There were no limits to what you could accomplish in this gym — that was the anthem playing on my heartstrings as I walked the shining floorboards.

Coach Lucero was in his office, and he handed over my shoes and suit. The shoes felt incredibly flat, without much cushion on the heel. The running shoes I wore as a child were regular department-store sneakers, and gave me some pretty nasty blisters, but after wearing them for a while they felt comfortable. I think what kept me safe from major injuries in those days was that I was lightweight and ran effortlessly. When I wore through the soles, I would cut out little squares of cardboard and slip them inside to cover the holes. (Of course, this wasn't much use in the rain — when the cardboard got wet, it disintegrated.) Compared to those old shoes, this new pair felt like solid gold. Still, turning them over in my hands, I began to feel nervous. Our first meet was only two weeks away. I knew a lot about running, but very little about cross country. I ran alone; competition was new to me. With adrenaline coursing through my body, I tried to remain calm as I walked to my next class. You're ready, I told myself. You'll be OK. The following self-assessment helped — and has tools you can use to calm yourself as well, if you start to doubt whether you have what it takes.

Runner's Self-Assessment

Ask yourself these questions (not necessarily in any particular order): Are you a good student? Are you mentally tough? Can you run in a variety of terrains? Can you adjust to adverse weather conditions? Above all, do you have a good attitude? This is crucial — attitude will make or break you. The positivity you bring to practice every day — and especially to race day — will be your greatest strength. Positivity carries over to every life situation. There will be days when you will have self-doubt. Turn off those feelings and put on a positive hat. You can do it! With the right attitude, you can accomplish any endeavor and overcome any obstacle.

Remember, no one is perfect. There will be times when things just don't go your way. We all have good days and bad days. What matters is how you cope with them. Let's say you arrive to practice unmotivated. We've all been there: You're just not feeling it. I wasn't always in a good mood on race day — everybody has ups and downs; sometimes that's just how the tortilla chip crumbles — but you have to be consistent if you want be a winner. Adjust your attitude, and you'll succeed.

Attitude is something you can get only from deep within yourself. Even though I might have felt unprepared to compete in an official cross-country meet, all my hours of training alone had one benefit: I learned to be my own support team, and my own competition. A good way to avoid negative thoughts is to think of running as a contest against yourself, and no one else. That's where attitude comes in. It can be a deep source of power and drive — cultivate it, nourish it and cherish it.

Powerful running comes from more than physical strength. Good runners have good legs and good minds — it's brain as well as brawn. Always strive to be the best that you can be, inside the classroom and out. Your contests won't only be won and lost on the field and in the gym. Remember, a loss isn't the end, and an error isn't a mistake until you refuse to correct it. I remember taking a pottery class when I was in seventh grade with Mr. Maes, the electronics teacher at the high school. He was an excellent teacher and very caring person, always demanding the best. He was the kind of person I call an "absolute:" firm in who he was, and always an advocate for those he mentored or taught. He'd help you find your hidden strengths — but then always demand the best from you. No slacking in his class.

One day the school principal, Mr. Melvin Cordova, left Mr. Maes a message that he wanted to see me in his office. "You are not doing well in pottery class, Gerry," he said. Mr. Maes always compared me to my brother Ben, who was an A student in his class many years back. Ben was a natural tinkerer, and very talented. Mr. Maes assumed comparing me to my brother would remind me of my own interior strength, as if greatness ran in the family. "Your brother was very good in electronics," he kept reminding me.

I promised Mr. Cordova to do better the next semester. "Okay, Gerry," he said. "I will be visiting you next semester to see how you are doing." That semester, we had a big project to complete, and I felt so much pressure to do well that I rushed around, made careless mistakes, and ended up flubbing it. I was floundering in the stormy seas of my own high expectations. Of course, Mr. Cordova stopped by Mr. Maes' class to visit on the very day our projects were due. We didn't have ashtrays at home, so I decided to make one. It was so misshapen, I might have been able to pass it off as a dinner platter instead. I was so disappointed. Still, the colors were okay —glazed in alternating light and dark blues — and that gave me a glimmer of accomplishment. I was prepared to toss the monstrous creation, but on the last day of class, Mr. Maes told the class not to throw anything out, even if we weren't happy with our work. "Leave them with me," he said. I left my plate behind.

Four years later, when I was a junior, Mr. Cordova had me come to his office. I couldn't understand why. "Please sit down, Gerry," he said with a smile. There on top of his desk was the ashtray I had made in Mr. Maes' class. It had been on his desk all this time. "I want to congratulate you on your running," he said, smiling and shaking my hand. Mr. Cordova became my hero that day. It truly opened my eyes to how grateful I was that he had not given up on me. I was deeply impressed by his kindness and interest in me. Mr. Cordova left the school the following school year, but he will always be the most unforgettable character I've ever met.

Finding strength within yourself can take the gentle reminders of a great mentor, like Mr. Cordova and Mr.

Maes. But you can also do it yourself, if you are mentally tough. Are you? If you have experienced pain — a cut on your finger, cold, or even the discomfort of waiting for someone to arrive — you have the prerequisites. You can develop mental toughness in your training by pushing your body to the limits: Go until you can't go anymore, and then push yourself a little more. If you can finish a race with nothing left in the gas tank, you have demonstrated mental toughness. Perhaps one of the most well-known examples of finishing a race with nothing in the gas tank is New Mexico's world class walker Jesse Castañeda who set a new world record for walking 300 miles non-stop.

My favorite sport to watch is boxing. Muhammad Ali is a good example of mental toughness. I saw him fight Smoking Joe Frazier for the heavyweight title in 1971. Ali had a 31-0-25 record, with 25 knockouts; Frazier's was 25-0-23. Frazier had a punch as strong as a mule kick and Ali was a punching machine. The fight was tough. By the final round, Ali was fighting with a broken jaw. Both men were exhausted, but still throwing punches. Frazier eventually won, but courage, endurance, and determination is a good example of mental toughness.

A runner can also develop mental toughness in practice. Far too often, I see kids jogging with their teammates to their training site, talking and laughing when they should be getting ready for the challenge ahead. Treat practice like

MY FIRST HIGH SCHOOL RACE

any other race. Made a pledge to yourself to give it 100 percent. If your coach tells you to run four intervals up a steep hill, run the last one as fast as the first. Make that promise before you even show up.

A cross country runner has to look forward to competition, no matter what. When we have the drive and passion to run, we run regardless of the weather. We can't sit and wait for ideal conditions. Again, consistency is key. Have you ever looked out the window on a very cold day and had second thoughts about going out to log your miles? It is not easy motivating yourself to leave your warm environment. It happens to the best of us, amateurs and elite runners alike. It's human nature. But you must put that first foot out the door. Indeed, take advantage of cold weather in practice so that on race day, if the weather is bad, you will already be conditioned to perform at your best, despite the conditions.

The same is true for terrain. Sometimes the course can be one long hill, like my first competitive race when I was in seventh grade (so anxious and excited to run, I barely noticed the steep incline!) Other times a course can cross into and out of many different kinds of geography. I ran a race in Santa Fe that started on flat terrain, then climbed up a long gradual hill, down the same hill into a sandy arroyo, then straight up and over a five-foot-high wall to finish with a lap around the track. A race like that hinges on strategy. I had to keep my opponent at least 15 feet behind me, in case I had trouble climbing over the wall.

In 2010, while training for the Duke City Marathon in Albuquerque, I went back to El Rito for an opportunity to reconnect with Forest Road 44. Forest Road 44 was more than just a quaint throwback to my childhood. It was a bit of a milestone, and I approached it with some tribulation.

Most of my training from seventh grade through high school took place in Canon de la Cueva, four miles north of El Rito on Forest Road 44. It's listed at 8,000 feet above sea level, but it has been reported as low as 7,400 feet. Forest Road 44 is not without its secrets — the dust above its dirty twists and turns holds stories of the countless feet that have traveled its winding path. If it could speak, you might hear it singing, "In rain, snow, hail, and thunder, through mighty winds and the hottest of days, Gerry was here, kicking up dust and paving the way for the next runner." My philosophy was, if dogs don't take a day off for Christmas, why should I? Cross country is a very short season, only four months out of the year. No sooner is the season over then it starts again. This means that you have to be a serious runner. You can't sit around waiting until the cows come home to get in shape.

MY FIRST HIGH SCHOOL RACE

Unchanged since I was in fourth grade, the road rolled along, sprinkled in various places with picturesque vegetation, like a dusty brown snake, flecked in emerald green, sidewinding on a long flat plane. The first landmark that I saw as I started running up the steep grade from the crossroads near the El Rito creek was the town's cemetery. As a young child, I remember passing the cemetery and thinking, just like those special people buried there had once had heaven in their sights, and fought and struggled and suffered but still kept hope alive, so too runners persevere, always looking ahead and never back. They lengthen their stride and run straight toward the goal to win. Further up the road, I got a clear view of a giant capital letter "N," identifying the name of the school (El Rito Normal School), that adorns the hillside in the Carson National Forest. (Today, the letter "N" has been replaced by a letter "E," for El Rito.) It was an annual tradition at the high school for incoming freshmen to paint the stones of the letter "N," like a freshman initiation by the senior class. Every fall, I'd see a stream of students flowing past my house and up toward the mountain, carrying rollers and large cans of white paint. The tradition was discontinued by the time I was in seventh grade. My cousins and I later raced up and down the abandoned route to the "N." And then I would come to the path where I veered off the road toward my grandmother's house, clouded with all the memories of those many visits. In my childhood, I would welcome someone slowing down on the road to tell me how fast I was running. Passing cars were rare in those days. Now, it's no longer an isolated road. The once lonely road now bustles with life. Outsiders come to El Rito to enjoy the wilderness. Once only dust from my running shoes puffed into the air; now the exhaust from cars leaves their stench of existence behind. But even when busy, Forest Road 44 holds thrills unlike any other trail for a born runner: dirt, hills and all. My days of running on Forest Road 44 instilled in me a passion and commitment that will never leave, and the thrill of it remains. The dedication and commitment I developed then has carried me so far in life; returning to the wellspring of that passion was a deeply moving experience.

Preparing For The Race

Of course, competition places unique demands on the serious runner, besides simply running fast. Even the best training can't prepare everyone for the mental stresses of a race. It is normal for someone to be nervous before a contest. I competed in the Duke City Indoor Invitational Track and Field Meet in Albuquerque when I was a freshman at Eastern New Mexico University. Sitting in my hotel room only hours before my two-mile

MY FIRST HIGH SCHOOL RACE

event, perspiration like streams of water through a dam began saturating my skin. I could feel the intense beating of my heart and the rising of pressure soaring to the top of my head almost made the room spin out of control. I felt like calling my coach and telling him, "Coach I can't run." Can you imagine how silly that might have sounded? Well, I ran and placed third behind Australian Kerry Pierce. (Pierce went on to shock the track world that year by setting a new indoor two-mile world record.) George Scott of Australia captured first with a time of nine minutes flat, with Pierce and me on his heels.

Sometimes stress triggers fear that leads to self-doubt: "What if I run out of gas during the race?" "What if I come in last?" This kind of thinking can defeat you even before the race starts. Racing is a competition with yourself. Just do your best! Still, there are ways to prepare yourself for the big day, mentally and physically.

What you eat the night before a race or in the morning for breakfast is a matter of personal choice. Some people suggest that you should not experiment with new meals or nutritional approaches, and I agree. Keep in mind the old running adage, "don't try anything new on race day." But I don't believe that there is a single ideal meal that everyone should eat. Eat what works for you, but I would suggest that you put something in your stomach in the morning so you won't feel hungry. Growing up, I didn't have much control over what to eat for dinner. I didn't eat junk food like soda, chips, or fast food — there were no fast food restaurants in my home town and no spending money to buy junk food at the general store. Instead, our regular dinner menu was a big pot of beans, a large fry pan of potatoes, fried in water, and a stack of wheat tortillas. Spinach was common in the spring. For desert, we ate baked apples. During the week for breakfast we ate oatmeal with powdered milk and a glass of water or powdered milk. On Saturdays, my father would make wheat-flour hot cakes. I would eat one for breakfast the day of the race, but sometimes I had the urge to eat more than one.

It can be hard to sleep before big events. This is not uncommon — but not at all welcome. A simple act turns challenging because of fear for what the approaching day will hold, the what-ifs and what-nots. My strategy was to socialize with my cousins to distract myself from the upcoming race. Obsessing over a race puts too much stress on you and drains you of energy you should conserve for the race.

Running The Course

Our first cross-country meet was going to be held at the high school next to the football field, and I had a pretty good idea about the design of the course. There

MY FIRST HIGH SCHOOL RACE

were no hills near the football field so I assumed the course was going to be flat. My childhood experiences had prepared me to run in any type of terrain or course design. The landscape was my coach, and I had plenty of adventures in the wilds around El Rito: walking on a log to across a raging river, racing my cousins up and down hills, running on sandy arroyos, swimming in the river (and almost drowning in a deep pond), climbing cliffs, riding on a run-away, four-wheeled, horse-drawn wagon and then jumping off just as the horses broke loose and the wagon crashed into a tree.

The El Rito course was flat and fast. It was generously decorated in the most picturesque vegetation, sage brush, cactus, and wild flowers. Rabbits and lizards scampered across the roads as we approached, low-flying birds humming to the rhythm of our feet. I hung back in the pack for most of the race and then moved up slowly. I was in third place as we approached the finish line. I could see the few spectators sitting on the bleachers that faced the football field. They were shouting words of encouragement but I couldn't hear them above the pumping of blood in my ears and the wind in the face as I ran. Exhaustion was forgotten; the stamina of my mind fueled my body forward, and with a strong kick I knew I could win. But ahead of me was Sofio, running in second place. My loyalty to my brother was at stake. Then the memory of Sofio chasing me in the alfalfa field flashed through my mind. When I outran him that time, he wasn't at all offended. We were brothers after all. I kicked into gear, hot on his heels.

I finished third behind Sofio. "Gerry, why didn't you pass me?" he asked. "Remember what I told you in the alfalfa field, that you were 'too fast?'" My love of my brother caught up to me — I could never outrun it. Still, Sofio said, I had to be faster next time. "I want you to run in Las Lunas and win," he said.

The distance from El Rito to Las Lunas was only 125 miles. It was a sunny day, about 80 degrees, with barely enough wind to blow a wildflower. I started getting nervous as we approached. People were assembled near the starting line. The entire scene was perfectly uniformed, and everyone was identifiable by their attire: Coaches proud in many-colored windbreakers, racers in their uniforms warming up with the famous runners' jig, shaking off the jitters through our arms, channeling peace and calm with nervous movement.

The course went up a flat-topped hill with a long steady climb over a quarter mile, then turned steep approaching the top with a 200-yard flat stretch before a gradual downhill for another quarter mile.

Minutes before the race, coach Lucero approached

MY FIRST HIGH SCHOOL RACE

me, put his right hand on my shoulder, and said, "That boy over there is the state champion. I want you to stay right behind him until you get to the top. Then pass him and run down as fast as you can." I was right on his heels at the start of the race. I wasn't going to take a chance and let him get away. A few yards to the top, the champion slowed down almost to a walk. He looked down the hill at me with an expression of intense and unprecedented panic that sent me soaring past him like a bolt of lightning. Sprinting ahead on the flat stretch, I prayed he wouldn't throw an unforeseen challenge my way. I had to get to the down-slope first, then run like a bat out of hell to the finish line. I didn't want to get into a neck-and-neck contest with this guy. He might have a good kick. One goal was on my mind: the finish line. There was no letting him get ahead of me.

Courtesy of El Rito Normal School

I could see coach Lucero waving his cap up and down over his head. Looking for that sign, his cap flapping up and down overhead, would be something that I looked forward to in all my high school races. My breath was short, my heart was pumping overtime, my legs felt shaky and weak, but his flapping cap made me feel good. I had won!

CHAPTER 3:

Training On Forest Road 44

Wild Horses Run Wild And Free

My uncle Mike loved horses and especially horse racing. Every summer, El Rito held a race for horses from our town and the neighboring villages during the Dia de Santiago festival. Uncle Mike never missed a race. I liked watching, too, and I'd run from my house to the fairgrounds on the outskirts of town to see the races, then hitch a ride back with him on his horse. I enjoyed talking with him. He was a walking encyclopedia on horse racing. One summer, before my seventh grade, Uncle Mike turned around as we rode and asked, "How would you like to see Kelso run?" "Who is Kelso?" I replied. "Only the best racing horse in the country. I found out today that he was named the U.S. Horse of the Year." I had to shout over the clip-clopping hooves: "If only I could catch one of those wild horses and race him against Kelso. My cousins tell me that wild horses are free." True, my uncle said, but "you would have to catch him first, then tame him, and train to run on a race track. Wild horses belong in the wild." I knew my uncle was skeptical of my plan, and protective of the wild horses' spirit, but I pushed him. "Who would win in a race, Kelso or the fastest wild horse in the wilderness?" We rode in silence as he thought about it. "Well," he said, "on a cross country course, the wild horse would win. Kelso would not be able to run up and down those hills. In fact, even if you train the wild horse, it might not run as well on the race track as it does in the wild because you would be taking him away from his habitat." I thought this over. What was my habitat? Was I wild and free? Uncle Mike pulled on the reins with a jerk, and we were home.

By the time seventh grade started, I had run halfway around the world — thousands of miles, back and forth on

Forest Road 44 — so I felt physically and psychologically confident about my running. I also had a feeling coach Lucero and I were a good match. Coach Lucero was a good listener and a truly genuine person. He didn't have personal experience as a distance runner, but he had the knowledge to guide an athlete toward his goals — he was a motivator. My brothers, Sofio and Pete had run for coach Lucero. Sofio was a member of his 1961 state cross country championship team. Sofio graduated the following year, but coach Lucero won team titles in 1962 and 1963 as well. He was a winner, and more importantly, he knew how to make winners out of his team. Coach was not as fortunate as some coaches in big city schools that welcome a stream of seasoned runners to the school every cross-country season. It was all from scratch, but he could harness raw potential for extraordinary results.

I knew I had found a gem in coach Lucero, but I didn't know what shape that gem would take — how would it fit into the jeweled crown I hoped would one day represent my running career? I was so used to training alone — what role would a new coach play? Coach Lucero didn't have the luxury of coaches in urban areas, where students were driven to and picked up from practices by adoring parents in big minivans. Our school was a boarding school, and some runners lived on campus while others were residents of the town. Each group had their own particular constraints. Townies often didn't have transportation to and from school at all hours, and boarders weren't allowed to leave campus. Time was also a constraint. Coach Lucero taught all day at the school, and had to manage all the responsibilities that came with that position, in addition to his coaching duties. Coach Lucero found another path. He used an "athlete-centered" approach to coaching, a method in which athletes take responsibility for their own training. This wasn't an alternative to traditional coaching — coach Lucero still had to keep track of the workouts, and runners were expected to report training data to him on a daily basis — but it helped him take a bit of a less intensive role in the process.

This coaching method was ideal for me because it didn't involve track workouts. Track workouts were a tough physical and psychological challenge for me, because the only training that I knew was on the roads around my rustic home. That was where I felt comfortable; running on a track was like being a country mouse in the big city. As my uncle said, I was a wild horse, and "wild horses belong in the wild so they can run wild and free."

Behind every successful runner is a great coach, and that certainly was true of coach Lucero and me. His coaching plan kept me fit year-round with cross country, basketball, and track. To improve my efficiency, coach

Lucero taught me proper arm swing, changing my form from an exaggerated swing to one with balance and rhythm. He encouraged me to warm up before races and warm down afterward. He taught me to set goals and pushed me to achieve them. More importantly, he taught how to make tactical decisions during big races.

In chapter one of this book, I wrote: "In the team, I'd cultivate this desire into passion and success." On coach Lucero's cross-country team, my running improved. During cross country season, coach Lucero entered me in as many cross-country races as possible; I ran not only in district meets, but in big invitationals too, where I had the opportunity to compete against runners from the big city schools.

During track meets, coach Lucero had me run the mile and 800 meters — this was effectively my track workout. The objective was to run those races as fast as possible, to teach my legs the pace, and ingrain it in my thighs and calves. Muscles don't forget. In some meets, I would run the anchor leg of the mile medley. During my senior year, we decided to sacrifice our chances of qualifying for state at the district meet by putting me in the open 800 meters instead of the medley relay. The mile team didn't qualify, but I not only qualified for state, but also set a new state record in the 800 meters.

My high school training program in high school was unstructured — freelanced, to put it another way — with almost no anaerobic training on the track. I was doing fartlek training, or "speedplay," based on the Lyiard system. (This is the coaching method that led Peter Snell to victory in the 800 at the Rome Olympics.) My training on Forest Road 44 started long before I was in high school, and progressed throughout my high school career. Every year I got stronger and stronger. A typical workout would start with a mile warm up of easy jogging from the school to Forest Road 44. Then I'd stop to stretch, and work through a series of short runs, long runs, and sprints. I used to make up the sessions as I went along, making sure not to run the surges too quickly. I had a trick to make sure I was pacing myself adequately: When I finished a surge, I would repeat the phrase, "Now is the time for all good men to come to the aid of their country." I knew that I was running too fast if I couldn't speak or understand what I was saying. Cool down was similar to warm up, without the sprints. I didn't run with a watch so I had to rely on markers like logs, boulders, earthen mounds, or trees and brush to judge distance and time.

Forest Road 44 bristled with abandoned logging roads that crisscrossed the mountain. These roads of medium to soft surfaces were great for fartlek training. Some ran for a mile, and then abruptly ended. I had to turn around and come back in the opposite direction, or find a connection with another logging road and then loop back to Forest Road 44.

Bob Kennedy, once the American record holder in the 5,000 meters, explains, "Any base period should include three components: gradually increasing mileage, the critical long run, and of course, at least one faster workout per week." Even without the component of speed work on the track, my long runs on Forest Road 44 consisted of speed strength to maintain a fast pace in my cross-country meets.

This simple fartlek training worked for me, but I was also active year-round, so I was fit and strong from lots of exercise. My year started with cross-country season, followed by basketball, then track. When I was not playing basketball, I was running on Forest Road 44. That explains why I couldn't dribble worth a damn, but I wanted to play basketball while still maintaining as much consistency as possible in my running.

The summer offered me more time to train and build aerobic strength. Some people map out new running routes to run to keep from getting bored. A change of scenery can help you stay alert and invigorated through the monotony of training. But not me. I ran on the same road from childhood to high school and never once got tired of it. In fact, just the opposite — my goal was consistency, and having the same route helped me stay focused, and built my mental toughness. John Wooden once said, "To be consistent requires a commitment on your part. It requires that you commit yourself to a sustained effort of action over the long-term. What this essentially means is that you keep your word to yourself and others that you will follow through with what you set out to do consistently over a period of time up until the moment your objectives are achieved." I made a commitment not to let any distractions creep into my training. This attitude led me to five state titles — I ran with the same passion and drive every time I stepped up to the starting line. Consistency was crucial; there were no such things as bad days. This meant running despite feelings of frustration, irritation, worry, and anger. I had to manage these emotions so they would not become distractions. That's not to say the world never intruded on my private sanctuary. I said before that Forest Road 44 was always changing — every run was unique — and the natural world would often break through the mental barriers I built to keep my own demons at bay. But I let it in. One time, I came upon a mountain cat, and chased it until it stopped, turned around, and faced me, challenging. I slowly moved away and escaped without incident.

    I was never bored. Many of us think boredom is just a fact of life, but in fact boredom isn't necessary at all. Boredom is a state of mind, and we can change our mental state through a redirection of attitude, by making peace with our present without living in an imagined future.

They say Peter Snell was surprised that he could run a sub-4:00 mile on the track just on fartlek training. He didn't believe that a simple routine was enough preparation for such a remarkable performance. Fartleks made me a fast runner, but I wasn't following coach Lyiard's system exactly, and my times in the mile and half mile were relatively slow. My best mile time in high school was 4:24. I ran the exact same time my junior and senior year at state. In comparison, Curry Hollis of Hobbs High School ran 4:09.8; Joe Espinosa of Silver City High School, 4:14; Ramon Leyba of Albuquerque High School, 4:19.1. Still, I ran against them in my senior year at the New Mexico High School State Cross-Country Championships, in separate divisions over the same course, and recorded the best time.

When I was a senior in high school, I would get tap water from a sink in the boys' locker room and rub it on my legs before going out to the starting line. My legs were white with flaky skin from washing at home in a galvanized tub, but I didn't have lotion, so water was a band-aid solution to the problem. My cousin Tito had the same problem. He also started rubbing water on his legs. One day a runner from another school came into the locker room while Tito and I were rubbing water on our legs and asked Tito, "What are you doing?" "Rubbing water on our legs." My cousin answered. "Does that help?" the runner asked. Without waiting for a reply, he too started rubbing water on his legs. Just then, five runners from another school came into the locker room and saw what we were doing. "What are you guys doing?" a runner asked. Tito didn't want to go into a long explanation, so he simply said, "It helps Gerry." They too, started rubbing water on their legs. There are no "short cuts" to improve your performance, no lucky charms to help you — only hard work.

It is important to remember the goal of training. It's not to run faster, but to run better. I always had the desire to play the guitar. My cousins all played the guitar and learning to play the guitar now is one way for me to keep their memory alive. They had one guitar in their home that was shared by everyone in the household. They couldn't afford to take lessons, but that didn't stop them, they learned to play the guitar by ear. Some time ago, I started taking lessons and have improved my skills. It is going to take time to get better. If you want to improve your running and get better, you are going to have to get internally motivated. If getting better is your goal. Nothing can stop you. Mental coaching is going to help. Surround yourself with positive thinking people. I am lucky. My guitar teacher is great at mental coaching. It's

TRAINING ON FOREST ROAD 44

not unusual to get an email once in a while that reads:

"Gerry, don't hold back sir, push yourself now – try to practice an hour a day, maybe pick it up twice a day for a half hour, whatever you are very close now to turning the corner on this thing and able to put it all together take your time, be patient, focus, make sure your right hand is playing the same string you left hand is on! Let me know how it goes, I am with you every step of the way. John."

Let me go directly to the point. To run better means to run consistently, to run smart, and to run strong. You don't have to be a sub-4 miler to win the New Mexico State High School Cross-Country Championships. If you can run a 5-minute pace through the 5,000 meter course, unaffected by the hills or the attitude, and finish strong, you will win. I did just that, and you can too.

One great advantage of my unstructured approach was that avoiding intensive track work kept me injury-free. This is probably the most important aspect of training and biggest concern of runners. Speed is important, but speed-work sessions are hard on the joints, and can often cause injuries. Especially one week before a championship

Courtesy of Eastern New Mexico University

race, I recommend staying away from doing activities in which you might get injured. Walking around the track is okay. Play defense, and take it easy — you're in excellent physical condition, and one week off of training won't hurt. In fact, it might save your race.

Author Lyiard

At Eastern, I majored in physical education. My freshman year, I took a physical education class with coach Babcock. The first day of class, coach asked me why I had decided to major in physical education. Because I wanted to coach like Author Lyiard, I told him. Lyiard was a New Zealand coach who had trained four Olympic medalists. He was my hero at the time, and still a major inspiration.

Coach Babcock incorporated much of coach Lyiard's system in his workouts, and built me a structured program while I was at Eastern. The aerobic base I had already established in high school prepared me for this more intense college-level training. Unlike my more independent high school approach, this structured training program required a lot of time with my coach. He had to be present at the training site, cheering his runners and keeping time. Coach Babcock told me that he was going to make me a sub-4-minute miler, but his real goal for me was to win the National Association of

TRAINING ON FOREST ROAD 44

Intercollegiate Athletics cross-country championships. He had passion for coaching coming out of his ears, and he worked my tail off. I tripled in one meet, running the mile (4:15), the 880 (1:55), and the three-mile (14:33). I remember finishing the mile and resting on the grass when coach walked by and said, "Gerry, the 880 is next." I had only 30 minutes to rest. I said, "I don't know why I feel so tired." He laughed and said, "I don't have the slightest idea." Of course he knew why — I was running as hard as I could. But I felt good. Coach Babcock pushed me beyond my limits. He had me run the Artesia, New Mexico marathon, and I placed second. According to the Lydiard method, the first training phase for any endurance race should be marathon conditioning. Some people think cross-country runners are tough, but I think it takes a tougher runner to run a marathon. The Artesia race was hard. I felt like dropping out, but around every corner of the course, coach Babcock appeared, cheering for me and calling out my time. A week after the marathon, he received a letter from someone in Artesia asking if I'd race against someone for a bet

Courtesy of Lamar University

— the writer bet I'd win in a backward 50-yard dash. We found the silly joke amusing. I didn't run that particular "race," but I ran many more under coach Babcock's watchful and supportive eye. Our hard work paid off: I placed fourth out of 320 runners at the NCAA meet in Wheaton, Illinois, qualified for the Olympic trials in the 10,000 meters, and placed first in a dual cross-country meet with the University of New Mexico.

That first-place finish came with a cost, though: I sprained my arch. Quoted in a Portales newspaper story about the meet, coach said, "Gerry was very much against missing the NAIA meet, but after conferring with several doctors, we decided it would be best not to let him run and take a chance of causing further injury. What started as a sprained arch during a dual meet with University of New Mexico several weeks ago has developed into a combination of sprained arch and bruised heel." Running is fun, but it causes pain too. You will get in shape, but it's going to hurt.

I finally met Lyiard during my senior year. He was 55 then. We had just run 15 miles from the Lamar campus to coach Babcock's house. Lyiard was a good friend of coach Babcock and had stopped in Beamont, Texas, to spend two days with coach and his family. He was drinking a beer from a can; I had a Dr. Pepper. "How did you get started running, Gerry?" he asked, taking a sip of his beer with one hand and using his other to wipe the sweat from his forehead with a napkin. "I ran an invitational cross-country meet and defeated the state champion, without any training." I said, hoping not to give Lyiard the impression that I was cocky. "You must have had a heckuva aerobic base," he said, putting his beer can back on the table. Needless to say, I was on cloud nine. "Gerry, if you win the NCAA National Cross-Country Championships, I will stop drinking beer and switch to Dr. Pepper," he said, smiling and shaking my hand. I don't remember how I got back to the campus that day, I was in such a daze of emotion and joy. I do remember well, though, the NCAA race: I finished in the top 25. Earning All-American status. An honor given annually to the best cross-country runners in the country.

In 1973, I was the guest speaker at the Southwest Track & Field Coaches Clinic in Grants, New Mexico. I was training for the 1976 Olympic Trials in the 10,000 meters and spoke at the clinic about the Lyiard system. The following year, I enlisted in the army and joined the all-army track team. In 1976, I qualified to compete in the 1976 Olympic Trails in the 10,000 meters. Coach Author Lyiard died in 2004 of natural causes at age 87. He was a huge influence on me and I hope I've kept his legacy alive and well through my success. I owe it all to him.

Mental Training

Physical training is important, but it is only one facet of the training you'll need to be a successful runner. The other piece of the puzzle — maybe its most important, in fact — is mental. Rigorous exercise of athletes' thoughts and attitudes is essential to improve their performances on the track, court, and field.

Some schools hold pep rallies to pump up students and fans and encourage athletes to perform at their best. We didn't have many rallies, but it wasn't unusual for coach Babcock to bring in a motivational speaker to talk to us before big meets. One of these speakers that coach Babcock invited was a banker. This guy was a fanatic about raw honey, and brought a big jar of honey and a loaf of wheat bread with him to our practices. Coach was convinced, and from then on he had us eat honey before practice. Motivational speakers like this were helpful because they weren't runners, and didn't talk to us about the race itself. Discussing strategies is not motivational; it only stresses out runners. I suggest that your coach schedule two meetings, one for planning strategy and the other for motivation. The strategy meeting should come first.

In 1967, while at Eastern, I competed in the Oklahoma State Cross-Country Jamboree. The Jamboree is one of the oldest and greatest cross-country races in the country. An outstanding field competes every year, with teams traveling from around the country to test their skills on the historic course. When I competed in 1967, I was racing against some of the best: Pat McMahon from Oklahoma Baptist was first at the 1966 National Association of Intercollegiate Athletics cross-country championships and John Mason of Fort Hayes State was second. Needless to say, I was nervous going into the race. But I knew I had to be in the right mindset. That required mental training. The night before the meet, all the runners were invited to dinner in a building on campus. We had a good meal and were shown an inspirational movie about running. It put me in a winning mindset. I was fired up. This is mental coaching. And it worked: At the Jamboree that year, I placed second behind Mason. McMahon was third.

Believing in yourself is crucial to achieving your goals. Without it, you'll never reach the top. And mental training is the nuts and bolts that help you obtain that mindset. Recently, my daughter came across an adage that read, in part, "If you ever go off the road, just make a U-turn and head back in the right direction." This might be something useful for you in life in general.

Someone who made a U-turn after suffering a setback in his life was Rutgers University football player Eric LeGrando. A tackle left LeGrando paralyzed from the neck down. His doctors assured him he would never breathe without a ventilator, but only five weeks later, he astonished everyone by drawing breath on his own. Eric never stopped believing in himself. He is still rebuilding his future in the face of hardship. A year after the accident, Eric joined his teammates in a home game against West Virginia during a snow storm. His triumphant return was awarded *Sports Illustrated*'s Fans Choice Best Moment of 2011.

If you want to be in the top five of your cross-country team, and your coach tells you that you have the potential — that's positive thinking, and great mental coaching. When I was a special education teacher working with children with learning disabilities, I made sure that my students perceived me — and the whole school community — as having high expectations of them. I made sure they knew that we had faith in them to achieve to the best of their abilities. A young seventh grader in my class was being bullied by a few other students about his physical appearance and became so distressed that he threatened to drop out of school. This student was bright, but his legs flexed slightly at the hips and knees, and he walked with his knees and thighs hitting or crossing in a scissors-like movement. In his book, *Winners Without Losers*, James P. Raltini argues that there is evidence that the way a student feels about himself and his ability to do schoolwork is positivity related to what he thinks others expect of him. I did everything I could to help this student *stop* focusing on the negative, and to think of the good things. I sponsored a play and gave him the leading role. I invited the school principal and other teachers in the building to my classroom to watch the play. The principal was so impressed that she scheduled an assembly to show the play to the entire school. Following the assembly, the bullying stopped. Subsequently, I was nominated for the Albuquerque Teacher of the Year Award. Five years later, I was visiting a high school in Albuquerque during lunch hour. As I walked across the parking lot, I heard someone yell, "Mr. Garcia! I want to be in your class." It was the same boy. He was now a senior in high school, in a long-term relationship with his girlfriend, and driving his own truck. He believed in himself.

Let's get you ready for the big race. Go to the nearest library or book store and pick up some motivational books. These books don't have to be about running; any sport will do, as long as there are stories of athletes succeeding *despite* the odds. Don't forget to pick up some movies about sport figures, too. Watch online clips of Olympic athletes you admire. Write your goal on a piece of paper and post it somewhere on the wall in your home where you can see it regularly, reminding yourself, "yes, I can!

And Don't Forget:

- The night before the big race, eat a good meal. No junk food like pizza, burgers, or fries.
- Go to bed early.
- Eat a light breakfast at least two hours before the race.
- Go to the bathroom.
- And good luck! "Yes, you can!"

CHAPTER 4:

High School, Eighth Grade State Cross-Country Champion

A Bad Race

It was just one of those days. My cousins and I were late. We had gone home for lunch, and would never make it back to school in time. Being late was one thing — being late for Mr. Espinoza, our math teacher, whose class was first after the lunch hour, was something else. Mr. Espinoza was tough, but a very good teacher. He had a good sense of humor and would always end his jokes by saying, "I am not trying to be fictitious." He was only 5'1," but a very burly looking guy.

I sprinted to the math building, and just as I made it to the door — *rrrrrrrrrip* — there they went. I heard the tell-tale tear, and felt a worrisome breeze on my rear. I had split my pants! I made a detour, and shouted at my cousin Frank, "Go to class! I have a pants malfunction." He dashed to class and I ran into the restroom to inspect the damage. My worst nightmare! I just knew Mr. Espinoza was going to call me to the chalkboard with part of my rear out there for everyone to see.

I walked into his classroom and sat in the back. My cousin Frank, smiled and waved me to my desk in the front row. I ignored him. When it was my turn to go to the chalkboard, I stayed put. "You, come to the board!" Mr. Espinoza said. I didn't obey, hoping he would call on someone else. "Come to the board or get out!" he said, so I walked out of the room. According to Frank, Mr. Espinoza told the class, "That kid is going to have a hard time getting back in class." The rest of the day, I walked with my hands in my back pocket hoping that people would either not notice or keep their comments to themselves.

I never went back. I dropped Mr. Espinoza's class and added business math with Mr. Jenkins. I knew I needed to take algebra to get into college, but I tried not to worry, hoping Mr. Espinoza would leave El Rito before my senior year. In rural areas, teacher turnover is common.

Mr. Jenkins was a tall, thin, quiet man, with eyeglasses and white hair. He was always neatly dressed in a white shirt and black tie. He was a very good friend of coach Lucero. The day before the state cross-country championships I visited coach Lucero at his apartment. Mr. Jenkins was there, too. During my visit, Mr. Jenkins asked me for my shirt size. "I'm not sure," I replied. "Come with me. I have some shirts that I want to give you," he said. We walked to his apartment, where I tried on ten very nice, long-sleeved white shirts. The sleeves were too long though, so we gave up and walked back.

The next day we got into the school's white, 1961 Chevrolet station wagon, and drove the hour and a half to Albuquerque for the New Mexico State high school Cross-Country Championships. The meet was going to be held on the north gulf course on the University of New Mexico campus.

This was to be El Rito's first appearance at the state championships, and we had a good chance of winning. The course was a two-and-a-half-mile loop. My plan was to stay hot on the heels of the defending champion. I knew him — I had defeated him last year as a seventh grader. Now he was a senior and we were going head-to-head again. When the starting gun went off, though, I forgot all about my former foe. Adrenaline surged, my nerves were ablaze. I was running somewhere in the middle of the pack when I snapped into focus and saw the state champion approaching a turn. I didn't even know that the finish line was right around the corner until I heard someone yell, "What are you waiting for!" It was my teammate, Sam Archuleta, catching up with me. He grew up in Truchas, in northern New Mexico, and was a member of the 1961 and 1962 state cross country championship teams and a fierce quarter-miler on our track team. I fired the afterburners, sprinted passed the champion, and won. We had also won the team title. Whenever I get recognized for that come from behind finish, I think of Sam. He helped me win.

Barely missing the finish happened to me again later that year at the state track meet. I was shoulder to shoulder with two other runners in the mile run with 200 meters to the finish line. I wasn't tired, but for some reason when they started to kick into higher gears, I didn't challenge. Max Varoz, a lifelong resident of El Rito, asked me after the meet, "What happened, Gerry? You could've won." "I don't know," I told him. "I wasn't tired, but I don't know why I didn't challenge for the lead."

I couldn't explain it. It was like a temporary freeze,

EIGHTH GRADE STATE CROSS-COUNTRY CHAMPION

a kind of paralysis. I remember feeling the same inexplicable, uncontrollable force once as a kid when my older cousins cajoled me to jump into a deep pond. My cousins and I usually swam around the inner edge of the pond, where it was shallow enough for us to stand up, but on that day, my older cousins convinced us all to line up on the diving board. I didn't want to jump, but something inside me made me leap. I hit the water and submerged. Buoyancy pulled me up, but when I tried to stand, I wasn't tall enough, and I went under again. My cousins Gilbert Jaramillo and Reyes Ortiz jumped in and rescued me.

It's safe to say that my first state race was not the best of my life. Racing isn't easy, especially as a beginner. Things will go wrong, but it's never too late to learn from past experiences. Experts agree that losses can fuel future wins, if you use them as opportunities to take stock of your performance and find areas to improve. With that advice in mind, I analyzed my performance.

Around that fateful corner was the finish line, but I didn't know it. The state champion had slowed down to a jog. He looked back at me and I saw the same panicked expression on his face that I remembered seeing when I passed him at the invitational meet in Lunas in seventh grade. How did this guy get ahead of me? There was no time to interview him — I sprinted past him and won.

I should've gotten out of the pack early and taken a position at the front. Most of the time, front runners win. Consider Grace Ping. Ping was a runner at Cotter Middle School in Minnesota, and a front-runner right out of the gate. She was the first seventh grader to win a cross-country state championship and took that momentum to burst onto the national scene with a big win at the Roy Griak Invitational, beating Judy Pendergast, the best distance runner in Illinois, and a senior to boot. Ping dominated the cross-country season, winning the conference and winning the state meet by almost a full minute. Still only fourteen years old, she ran in the Nike Cross-Country Nationals in Portland, competing against the nation's best high-school athletes. Unfortunately, after such early success, Ping moved with her parents to Park City, Utah, where ULFSAA rules did not allow an eighth grader to compete in the state high school championship, leaving us to only imagine the heights she could have reached.

But starting out fast has a risk: you can hit a wall and run out of gas. If you are not confident you can lead the pack, stay inside and conserve your juice. You might come from behind to win the race at the last second in a stunning finish.

What can I do to next time? You can build mental

EIGHTH GRADE STATE CROSS-COUNTRY CHAMPION

strength by pushing yourself in practice beyond your limits. You'll know when you reach that point because your body will be crying like a baby — but you have to keep going! At Eastern New Mexico University, all our cross-country workouts ended with a 100-meter sprint. This wasn't for our legs as much as our minds. The point was to psychologically condition us to run fast even when we were tired. Every day I had to literally drag myself to the starting line, I was so beat. But I still gave that sprint 100 percent, following through on the pledge I made before coming to practice. I pushed myself in that sprint by trying to defeat my roommate Fred. Fred Sandoval was a star sprinter at Cuba High School, and a state champion in both the 200 meters and 400 meters.

I also analyzed my performance at the NCAA National Cross Country Meet in New York in 1969. I studied a map of the course with coach Babcock, but didn't have time to walk it before the race. Still, I wasn't concerned about getting lost. The course was a narrow trail bordered by trees on both sides. Two hundred and fifty-four of the best collegiate runners in the country were running in this meet: Gerry Lindgren, 1966 and 1967, NCAA cross country champion; Michael Ryan, winner of the 1968 NCAA cross country championship; Steve "Pre" Prefontaine, the "prodigy" who had just started his freshman year at the University of Oregon; and many

Courtesy of Track & Field News

sub-4 milers.

The Van Cortland Park cross-country meet had a reputation for having one of the toughest courses in the nation. Runners crossed a flat, grassy field to the first turn, 400 meters from the starting line, then merged onto a rocky, ankle-twisting, six-mile, narrow trail up and down hills through the woods, until they popped out to sprint across a 200 meter flat stretch to the finish line.

My coach told me to start fast to avoid getting boxed in when the pack entered the single track in the woods. I ran well at first. I remembered being told that long distance races are never won in the first 400 meters—they're often lost there. I reached the turn ahead of the other runners but I could hear the heavy breathing and crushing gravel as the runners closed in on me from behind. I heard, "Go Pre!" A thought popped into my mind. Prefontaine must be getting ready to take the lead. I had to make a smart tactical decision. Stay on his heels or run my own race. I was confident that I could run against anyone. Then Prefontaine went flying past me, followed by a group of eight or nine runners.

The pace was fast. It looked like a tactical battle. A surge was happening early in the race and I decided to let them go. I was hoping the leaders might run themselves off their feet before the finish, but they established a gap that was maintained throughout the race. It was a crazy scene, a chaotic swarm of arms and legs bouncing up and down through the wooded trail. There was no time to settle down. Runners continuously passed each other back and forth.

At some point in the race, I realized the pace was increasing drastically. I could hear the sound of people at the finish line. Before I knew it, I was looking down a small, steep hill at the finish line flags.

I noticed Bob Gray from Arkansas State approaching the bottom. Bob had defeated me at conference when he pulled off the upset over me with a surprise sprint. A neck and neck race with him again would not be good. The last 200-meter stretch was flat and fast. I stampeded alongside a crowded field of runners to the line, running shoulder to shoulder. There was no podium to race for. Finishing strong was my only goal today. I placed a humble twenty-third. Gary finished in 25th place, just barely making the cut-off for All-American status.

What did I do wrong? I could've known what the halfway point looked like had I checked the course before the race. Knowing that the finish line was near would've propelled me to the line with every ounce of strength that I had in me and did not know that I had.

Gerry Lindgren won the race. Lindgren would write later, "I went through the mile in 4:06. Prefontaine was back in the pack at 4:15." In an article shortly after the race, race officials included my name in a short list of runners to be on the lookout for next year. I didn't compete the following year because I graduated from Lamar.

After the meet, coach Babcock told me, "Leonard is devastated that he didn't make All American." Leonard told Babcock, "Gerry did something that I have been trying to do for four years." Leonard is the only University of Houston runner and first Texan to break the 4-minute barrier in the mile; he attained the feat 32 times. After completing his running career at Houston, Hilton placed third at the U.S. Olympic Trails to run in the 1972 Olympics in Munich, Germany.

Leonard passed away from pancreatic cancer at 52.

Defying The Odds

In my freshman year, coach Lucero invited several other

schools to our first cross-country meet in El Rito. It wasn't the same course I had run in seventh grade — similar, but not the same. The course was flat and fast. We had to run from the school football field across the gym's parking lot, across the campus to my old elementary school, around an open field near the El Llano cemetery, across the parking lot again, and over the last 100 meters to the finish line in front of the football field bleachers. I covered the 1.8-mile course in 8:47:05. The coach of one of the other teams argued that I must have cut the course because my time was too fast. When coach Lucero invited the same schools later in the season, he made sure that the coach who had complained about my performance was invited too. He had his fans stand at each marker along the course to make sure I didn't cut. I ran three seconds faster the second time, finishing in 8:40. The coach was heard saying later, "that kid is fast!"

(I wore spikes for this meet. The kind of shoes you wear for a meet — flats or spikes — is a judgment call. Base your choice on what kind of surface you will be running on. Your coach can help you decide, but it should be your decision; after all, you will be doing the running. I decided to wear spikes because most of the course was flat dirt and I wanted a fast time. But with spikes on, I had to be careful not to slip and fall when the course changed to asphalt. I knew that running on asphalt was going to be rough on my feet. Generally, you should wear flats for long distance races.)

At the state cross-country championship that year, we won our second straight state team title, defeating second-place Fort Wingate. A chilling wind gusted fitfully, but I felt good going into the race. The meet was on a golf course. There were no crossovers or switchbacks — it was all one, continuous two-and-a-half-mile loop with barely any hills. I decided to wear my spikes since there was a sand trap about a mile before the finish line. We had to run on a narrow, flour-lined path alongside the sand trap, then make a sharp turn to continue to the line.

As the reigning state champion, I knew everyone was gunning for me. I went out fast and took the lead. One advantage of being an aggressive front runner is that most of the time you run alone for the entire race. Sometimes, someone will hang on with you and then fade. A runner from Fort Wingate ran on my heels, but faded with one mile to the finish line. He slowed down and I zoomed away, disappearing in the distance to win my second straight state cross-country title.

My victory at state as a ninth grader was historic because it is very rare for an eighth grader to repeat as state champion. Most successful eighth grade runners let the pressure get to them. All eyes are on them to win.

I was a little taken aback by the attention at first, but

my parents had worked hard to keep me grounded even if others told me how a good runner I was. I didn't have narcissistic parents. They were supportive and tried to shield me from too much outside hype. One day I was walking through the dining room when I overheard a man talking to my dad. "Is that the fast one?" he asked my father. My father didn't answer. "Have you raced him against runners from other states?" asked the man. "No just here," my father replied, and quickly changed the subject. Beginners often succumb to pressure from their parents, or other sources. I am a prime example. When my daughter was three months old, I bought a baby stroller and logged many miles with it. I was hoping to get her interested in running. I ran with her in the baby stroller until she was six years old.

I spent the next three years watching my daughter while she trained in karate. When she was ten, I registered her with the Youth Track Club, a running club for children 5 to 18. A few weeks into practice, she came home sad because a coach in the club had criticized her for showing a lack of motivation. The coach later explained to me, "She does not want to be here; she is doing it for you." This was quite a wake-up call. Was I pushing and pressuring her into something she didn't truly love? I had my daughter finish the season, but she soon lost interest in sports all together. My daughter's interest is writing, not sports. I learned this, and let her pursue her passions on her own. Today, she is in the Honor Program in college studying to be a writer. Still, she jogs for fun — and I take some joy in that!

Taking Defeat In Stride

My sophomore year, I suffered my first defeat in two years. Coach Lucero inadvertently took a wrong turn on the way to the race, and we arrived at the meet with the starter's pistol already pointing to the sky. Someone near the starting line yelled, "El Rito is here!" We ripped off our warm-ups — no time for that! — got in line, and were off and running. With no time to stretch before the race, my hip flexors felt tight. I had been sitting in coach's car for the long ride to the meet, and now I could hardly move, running in slow motion. I finished second. I congratulated the winner from Sandia High, put my warm ups back on, and waited for my teammates to finish. It was a nightmare. The next day a short article in the Albuquerque Journal read: "Schuch Beats Gerry Garcia." I had my revenge, though: At the New Mexico State Cross-Country Championships a few months later, I ran a faster time than Schuch to win my third straight title.

After cross-country season, I joined the school's

basketball team. I was home for lunch when I heard the news on the radio that President Kennedy had been shot. We had an assembly after lunch to honor him. That night, we had a game with Pecos High School, a town about 82 miles from El Rito. I didn't feel like going on the road trip. I guess I was traumatized like everyone else in the country. Benny Trujillo, a boy that lived about a mile from my house on Canyon Road, was also on the basketball team. He was a junior. I had seen him around town, but I didn't know him very well. When I was younger, his grandfather would pass my house on his way home and say, "Se me olvido, pero cuando nos encontramos otra ves, te doy un manojo de bolitas." (I forgot, but next time we meet, I'll gave you a bunch of marbles). One day, he brought me a hand full of marbles — just like he had promised. Benny and I became good friends. His mom would give us a ride home after basketball practice. We shared a seat in the school bus on out of town games.

There was continuous coverage of the assassination of President Kennedy that night on the school bus radio. It was annoying. Benny and I didn't discuss the assassination. We chatted like kids. I told him about an experience I had when I was eight during the Dia de Santiago celebration. I saw two men fighting each other outside the dance hall across the street from my house. I ran to tell my mother. "Beber alchohol afecta el pensamiento," she said — alcohol impairs your thinking. It was a quick lesson on why not to drink intoxicating beverages.

Benny told me about an experience he had at the Dia de Santiago as well. "I ran a race and won a prize," he said. "How old were you?" I asked. "I don't remember, maybe nine or ten. But I do remember that I edged out a skinny, dark-skinned boy to win first place," he said. "What!" I yelled. "That was me!" He covered his face with both hands and said, "O my God!" We laughed all the way to Pecos. We were buddies, and teammates as well. Benny was a sprinter, and we complimented each other's running skills. He and I were in the mile medley that broke the state record my junior year. He ran the first 200-meter leg, and I anchored the relay with an 800-meter run.

Sometimes after a long run, I would join Benny when he was practicing getting out of the blocks. He would get into his sprint position and I would take a standing start. We would come out of the blocks even, but a couple of strides later, he would pick up speed and leave me in the dust.

Benny died in a tragic accident in the winter of 2010 in Santa Fe, New Mexico. According to witnesses, Ben ran onto a frozen pond to rescue his dog. The ice broke and Benny fell into the freezing water and drowned.

Coach Vince Martinez — "Marty" — was the head

coach of the basketball team and coach Lucero was his assistant. Coach Martinez had coached the team that had won the state high school championship in 1957. I didn't play much in games, but I didn't mind. I felt honored to play. Besides, coach Lucero wanted me playing basketball to stay in shape for track season.

In college, I ran year-round: cross-country, indoor, and track. When cross-country season came around again, I was ready to compete. Staying in shape year-round is important for cross-country runners, but so is rest. Overtraining can lead to injury. Taking a couple of weeks off after the season is a good idea. Then again, no activity is without risk. I learned that the hard way on the basketball team.

High school basketball was a high-level competition sport, and that meant injuries. It was rough. Early in the season, in a game with Pecos High, I got my nose broken. Coach Martinez took me to the doctor the next day, and my nose was repositioned. The doctor told me I could keep playing, as long I stayed out of trouble — and kept away from the key, or the space just beneath the basket, for the rest of the season. I resumed practicing with the team. One day, I went to retrieve the ball from just outside the free throw line, and — bang — got hit in the nose again. I didn't bother going to the doctor this time; it healed by itself, but had to have surgery years later to fix a blocked airway.

High school basketball wasn't particularly fun. Games were too intense and competitive, but I enjoyed the workouts. The full-court man-to-man press defense was my favorite. Running in basketball is much different than cross country. Basketball requires you stop and go. In cross country, if you stop, you fall behind. I was out of my comfort zone, but I think that made me a better overall athlete. If you're given the chance to try a new sport, go for it, even if you're not used to the exercises. You might learn something.

Comeback Kid

In my junior year, I suffered another defeat at the second annual Albuquerque Invitational. Car trouble this time: a broken fuel line. We arrived at the meet mere moments before the start of the race. I had only a few minutes to warm up. Warm up had always been a personal responsibility. I had been taught that warming up before a race should be part of planning. Without a good warm-up, you can't have a good performance. Warming up doesn't just get your legs ready for action; it can prevent injuries. Coach Lucero would always try to arrive at the meet at least one hour before start time to warm up. At the Albuquerque meet, though, I only had time to jog back and forth a little before I had to line up

EIGHTH GRADE STATE CROSS-COUNTRY CHAMPION

for the start. The gun went off and we were on our way.

It was a tactical race from the start. A runner from a bigger school set a fast pace. My legs felt like a limp rubber band. He won; I was second. Later, at the New Mexico State Cross-Country Meet, he tried the same strategy and it backfired. He hit the wall. I saw him face down on the dirt as we were leaving. It reminded me of the Sloveian ski jumper, Vinko Bogtaj, competing in the 1970 International Ski Flying Championship in Oberstdorf, West Germany, when he tumbled over the edge of the ramp during his take off and flipped wildly, almost landing on the spectators. It was all caught on film for Wide World of Sports. Jim Mckay described the action in his signature style: "The Agony of Defeat." It looked bad, but, thankfully, Bogtaj wasn't injured and continued competing in ski jumping.

I thought of this seeing the runner there, totally spent, in the dirt. "The Agony of Defeat." He had had a chance to celebrate when he defeated me; now it was my turn. Not only did I beat him, but I ran the fastest time of all the divisions. Tables always turn in the wide world of sports. One minute you're up, and the next you're down. How well can you handle the thrill of victory and the agony of defeat? It wasn't easy for me to accept that I had been defeated. I internalized my stress. I may have seemed perfectly fine on the outside but I was a mess of emotions on the inside. However, I was determined to make a comeback, so I tried to spend my time visualizing myself winning, rather than thinking of the loss.

George Forman is a good example of a comeback kid. These days, he is the guy in the commercials selling grills. But Forman was a heavyweight boxer in his time, and an Olympic gold medalist at the 1968 games in Mexico. Later he turned professional. In 1973, he knocked out Joe Frazier to win the title. Frazier had defeated Ali in 1971. The next year, Ali fought Forman and knocked him out. Forman was devastated over the loss, but didn't give up his boxing. In 1977, George Young defeated Forman by UD in round 12 of 12. Forman was so devastated that he retired from boxing and became an ordained minister. In 1994, Forman, out of shape from so long out of the ring, was given a shot at Michael Moorer, 19 years his junior, for the heavy championship of the world. Forman, then 45, knocked out Moorer to become the oldest fighter to win the World Heavyweight Championship.

You can be a comeback kid too. You must have passion. How hungry are you to succeed? Maybe you want a shot at making the school's cross-country team. Maybe you want to win a medal, or just run a personal best. Maybe your comeback is something off the track or outside the ring. Don't give up! You can do it.

CHAPTER 5:

Five Straight High School Championships

Crisis At Home

The summer before my senior year began under stormy skies. Our home was racked in crisis. Sofio was suffering from schizophrenia and had barricaded himself alone in an empty room in the house. He'd emerge suddenly, only for food, then retreat to his private dungeon. He spoke to no one, wore an ankle-length coat, and had unkempt hair and a wild beard.

I barely recognized him. When I was a child, Sofio was my constant companion. I was a bundle of nerves the day before I started high school and Sofio calmed me down with a story making fun of himself when he was that age. "I was in the gym's locker room, when I heard Coach Marty yelling for everyone to line up in the gym for calisthenics. I couldn't find my gym shorts so I ran out in my underwear. 'Hey! Sofio, get back in there and get dressed!' Coach demanded, and followed me into the dressing room with a pair of gym shorts." I could picture the scene — it was a hilarious story, and lightened my mood, readying me for the big day. But now, this calm and kind protector had vanished.

Sofio was also very intelligent. He was the first of my family to go to college right after high school, but unfortunately he dropped when he couldn't afford the books. One of his professors, impressed at his talents and sad to see him in financial stress, offered to buy the books for him, but Sofio refused to return to school. Later, he confided in me that he couldn't concentrate. His mental illness was taking its toll, and beginning to warp his brilliant mind. After that, he gradually drifted into a world far removed from the one we know.

Ensconced in his fortress, Sofio resisted all help, but I was defiant. He was not going to fight this illness alone. I would break down his walls of madness, and find a cure.

I would find the right drug for him. If anyone was going to persuade him to get help, it was going to be me, but first I had to convince him to talk. I had an idea. What if instead of trying to make him believe that the voices he heard were not real, instead, I convinced him that they *were*, and then form an alliance with him to get rid of the intruders through medication? It was worth a try. I felt optimistic. I was thinking like a winner. I would give this new goal every ounce of strength I had, every drop of sweat, as if it were any other athletic challenge. Whatever it took — I would not give up.

The day I was going to try out my idea, my cousin Tito stopped to visit and to invited me to go to Colorado with him, his brothers, and my best childhood friend, Hilbert Archuleta, for the summer to weed the agriculture fields in Capolin, a small town 65 miles from El Rito. "Gerry, you need to take a break away from running. It will do you good," he said. It was interesting to think that some people live in the hustle and bustle of the big city, only to escape to a small town for a relaxing getaway, while I was going from one small town to another, smaller one, to work in the fields. "Well, I guess you're right," I said. We all find relaxation somewhere — the key is to change, and adapt to our new surroundings. Even if it's just another small town. Maybe working and not running would be a welcome diversion for me. So the next day I packed up, and soon a van arrived at my house and we headed to Capolin.

In mid-summer, I left Capolin to start training in El Rito. Sofio's precarious situation weighed heavy on my mind as I rode back to El Rito with my boss, who kept me entertained the best he could, steering our wide-ranging conversation to diverse topics like politics, careers, and life. Soon enough, we arrived in El Rito. I thanked my boss, he hung a U-turn, and headed back to Colorado in a cloud of New Mexico dust. I was on a mission as I walked through my front door, but my father stopped me in my tracks. "Geronimo, I have some sad news about your brother," he said. Sofio had disappeared without a trace. I reeled from the announcement, lost in thoughts of disaster. A demon must have penetrated his mind and completely taken over! I realize now that this was ridiculous — Christians can't be possessed, and demonic possession isn't the same thing as mental illness, I kept reminding myself. The county sheriff was notified and began to look for him. Meanwhile, I searched in all the places in the mountains he and I had visited, but couldn't find him. The local radio station informed the public, but he didn't turn up. I started to lose hope. Then one day, after he had been missing for about a month, a miraculous turn of events: I heard on the news that Sofio had been found alive. St. Jude had answered my prayers. He was home and safe. A man fishing outside of town found him wandering the headwaters of the river, twenty miles away. According to this man, Sofio was running, stumbling, and falling along El Rito Creek, trying to catch fish with his hands. He was rescued!

I raced home as soon as I heard, and ran into the house with open arms. The first thing I did was hug my brother, but he only stared at me, puzzled. "You're supposed to be dead," he said. "They killed you." He was in bad shape. His clothes looked like they had been through a grinding machine. His tennis shoes were hanging on his feet by a thread. And this nonsense about my death? He told me he was in a tree one night, and I was trying to convince him to climb down when a group of men with machine guns showed up and killed me.

Sofio recovered from his ordeal, but was ill for the rest of his life. Thankfully, his condition improved in residential care in Las Vegas, New Mexico. I'd visit him there every other weekend. In the winter of 2005, I was planning to visit Sofio on Christmas Eve, but the roads to Las Vegas were impassable, so I postponed my visit until Christmas. That night, Sofio died suddenly from an abdominal aortic aneurysm. He was a warrior till the end, and suffered his traumas with stoic grace. He was a true winner. He never complained, and ran the race of his life with strength, endurance and power right till the end. I remember him fondly.

Praying In Church

It was my first day of senior year. I was looking over my schedule for the semester, and still had space to add algebra. I had to take algebra to get into college, but Mr. Espinoza had kicked me out of his math class in eighth grade and probably didn't want me back. I didn't know what to do. One night, beset by anxiety, I just couldn't sleep. I decided to sneak out of the house at midnight to pray at the church. I had to be careful to make sure my father did not see me. I knew he'd be awake, and patrolling the yard. Not in vigilance, but by necessity: We didn't have an indoor toilet, and my father's diabetes was getting worse, so he had to go to the outhouse every half hour to relieve himself. I silently snuck outside. It was a cool, moonless, windy night, with a sky full of stars. I stood in the backyard. To the left of me was Pat Martin's alfalfa field, where I would ride with Pat on his tractor and where Sofio had chased me as a kid. The tall alfalfa grass in the field, gently moving back and forth by the wind, looked like dark ocean waves.

Fifty yards ahead was a dilapidated, abandoned adobe house, a victim to the ravages of time and weather, its large windows long knocked out, its floors rotted, its walls bare. It had been empty for as long as I could remember. Next to it was an abandoned garage with a pitched roof, boarded windows, and two large barn doors. A lady in town claimed a man dressed in a blue suit and tie stood in the entrance to the garage to watch her as she walked home from church. It was a vision of guilt for something she had done, or failed to do.

This is her story. Three young residents of El Rito were intoxicated one night and riding in a car down a windy road coming from Ojo Caliente, a small village twelve miles from town. The driver failed to negotiate a curve at the bottom of the hill and rolled, spilling all three occupants. The driver was in critical condition, and the other two suffered minor injuries. The driver was loaded into another car to take him to a hospital in Espanola, thirty miles away. On the way, they stopped at this particular young lady's house. He begged her for water but she ignored him. He died on the way to the hospital. She felt guilty — this vision was his ghost. I remembered this as I walked. The night breathed menace. Memories of misdeeds, regrets, and painful pasts loomed. I was scared and nervous as I approached the church.

The first house on the left side of road was well maintained, but empty, as if the owners had walked out of it and never returned. The story I heard when I was a child was that an elderly lady lived there alone. She had gotten frustrated with her life and went around town telling people she wished she was dead. One day she was diagnosed with an incurable illness. She had only a few days to live. She had a change of heart, asking God to spare her life, but she soon died.

In another house lived an elderly lady, alone. She was the grandmother of my childhood friend, Max Marquez. She would hire me on occasion to chop wood for her and stack it in her house. Across the road from her was a big, two-story house, still livable, but empty. Three friends of my brother, Pete, claimed it was haunted. One night when they were in high school, they slept over in the house. All night, creepy noises kept them awake. Squeaky sounds like someone walking on a wooden floor, and doors opening and closing on dirty hinges. As I came around the corner, flashes passed through my mind of the times my cousins and I played chicken dares to see who could spend more time inside the house at night.

I walked toward the church through a rock-walled courtyard. The church was camouflaged by the darkness of the night. All I could see was the white cross on the steeple, pointing to the heavens. I made the sign of the cross as I walked by the grave yard. One marble stone marked where a priest had been buried, long before I was born. He had crashed head-on into a semi-truck on his way to a church in Ojo Caliente. Exactly who was responsible for the accident was not clear.

I pulled the door to the church open, walked across a small room and pushed gently through two swinging doors to the nave. It was dark, without a sound. A beautiful smell permeated the still, warm air. A small red light on the altar, empty of sacred images of saints, was the only illumination. Only the statue of the Virgin Mary and Jesus on the cross and some paintings were left.

All was silent. I felt watched. After all, this was Jesus' house. I dipped my index finger into a container of holy water, made a quick bow toward the alter and then walked up a short staircase to the balcony, where the parents of my childhood friend, Leroy Salazar's, both blind from birth, would play the organ and sing at Sunday mass when I was growing up. At the top of the staircase I could see the rope to the church's bells, hanging like a lifeless snake. When I was in second grade, I tried pulling the rope to ring the bells, and the movement pulled me up from the floor until I let go and landed safely on my feet.

I knelt facing the alter, made the sign of the cross, and prayed. "Jesus," I said, "you knew that I was coming here tonight. I have never prayed to win a race and I will never do so. My fifth grade teacher, Mr. Anecito Varoz used to say, 'Where there is a will, there is a way.' Jesus, I need you to guide the way for me. I need to take algebra to get into college." I made the sign of cross and ended my prayer. I slowly walked down the staircase, made the sign of the cross again, bowed toward the altar, and existed the church. I sprinted to my house, dogs barking, as if cheering me on. I waited for my father to go back inside, then climbed through the window into my room and went to bed.

The next day at school, coach Lucero stopped me in the hall and said. "Gerry, I need to talk to you." He gently guided me to the wall, rested his hand against it and placed the other hand on my shoulder. "Gerry, you need to take algebra. I have gotten to know Mr. Espinoza well and he is a very friendly person. He wants you back in class. He has already told the other kids that you are coming."

I was nervous taking algebra with freshmen, but as I walked into the room, no one seemed to notice, except for two students who looked up at me and smiled. They were Tony Chacon, a good friend of mine who lived close to my grandmother's house, and Grey Martin, the son Tom Martin, the owner of the general store across the street from my house.

The Fifth Time's The Charm

It was all over the news: Tomorrow was going to be the New Mexico high school state cross country championships in the Albuquerque foothills. But to me, it was just another day. It was my senior year and I was determined to win my fifth consecutive state title. I had taken a vow of abstinence from running for a week before the championship, a philosophy shared by coach

Lucero and I as a key component to staying injury-free. We believed that I would be in peak psychological and physiological shape come Saturday's meet. I must admit, it was a challenge not to run, and sometimes I had the uncontrollable urge to run just one fast lap around the track. Denying myself something that I enjoyed doing reminded me of Lent when I was a child. My brother Ben knew how much I loved to run and one day during Lent asked me, "Geronimo, are you giving up running for Lent?" I just smiled and shook my head. As a child, I grew up thinking that not giving up something for Lent was a sure path to hell or purgatory. "Ah, don't worry about it, Easter doesn't have to be only about religion. In ancient times, the Greeks would celebrate Easter with races," he said, smiling.

Curry Hollis of Hobbs High School was the favorite to win the 6A division. Curry and I had had similar childhoods. We were both the same size: skinny, with skinny arms and legs. I was dark complexioned with black hair and Curry was lighter skinned with blond hair. He was born to a humble family in the small town of Artesia, New Mexico and later moved to Hobbs, where he attended school. Jay Mason, a track star at Hobbs High School, would write later that Curry showed up for cross country wearing very poor running shoes, so the team all pitched in to buy him a good pair. From that day on, Curry was unbeatable. I was favored to win the small division. Curry had run the mile in 4:09.8 at the Golden West Invitational Meet. His time in the mile run is still the state high school record.

I was standing close to the finish line with my friend and former teammate, Billy Trujillo, as the crowd roared its approval of Curry sprinting to the finish line to win in 9:49. When it was my turn to run, I went out fast and left the pack behind. From the top of the first hill I could see a stream of runners gradually the hill. I set a fast pace and sprinted to the finish. My time was 9:41!

I ended my cross-country and track high school career by winning the mile and the 800 meters at the state championships later that year. I set a new record in the 800 meters. The day after the meet, a photo of me and coach Lucero ran on the front page of the Albuquerque Journal.

The assembly at the high school to honor my victories was the highlight of my career. I remember the day well: Students filtered into the gym, laughing softly, smiling, and talking in quiet, barely audible voices. Teachers followed, watching for any act of misbehavior. I walked into the gym and stood next to a large podium with microphone. I started my speech by thanking coach Lucero. "I'm so grateful for everything you have done in these past years to help me out. You remind me of

Mr. Novak," I joked [he was a famous teacher on TV at the time]. "Thank you for teaching me how to set goals and how to achieve them. I don't know what I would do without your support."

Then I thanked the student council and the students. "Thank you so much for the generous gifts, the luggage, waist watch, and money. What a treat! You all have truly touched my heart. This award recognizes not me alone, but the whole school and school community, present and past. Without you, none of this would have been possible."

After I finished my speech, the students filed out of the gym. Many shook my hand. A few girls wiped tears from their eyes.

In the library of a branch of Northern New Mexico Community College in El Rito stood a trophy case, and on one shelf rested a pair of bronzed running shoes. Coach Lucero paid me a great complement my senior year in high school when he bronzed the track shoes that I wore following my fifth state title. My high school closed in 1969 and the college shut down in 2015.

College And Beyond

Several colleges, including track powerhouse Kansas, showed an interest in me, but I chose Eastern New Mexico University. During my first semester at Eastern, I wrote a letter to my brother Ben, who was in the Navy. He told me that he was studying electronics. He was one of fifteen servicemen enrolled in an electronics course. The top six of the class would participate in a special project. When he was chosen for the project, I was elated. But he was self-conscious about his achievement. "The others in the class look at me as if I have a big head," he wrote. I wrote him back, but he didn't reply. I was scared for him, and nervous. What explained the silence? It turned out, he had suffered a nervous breakdown. In 1993, Ben died in a residential home when the staff accidentally gave him a double dose of medication. He was 55.

I only stayed at Eastern for one year. During my sophomore year, my coach took a job at Lamar University in Beaumont, Texas, and I followed. After graduating from Lamar, I came back to Albuquerque. I couldn't find a job, so I took a special education class at the University of New Mexico. My professor was also the principal at a school for trainable, retarded children in the city. She hired me to work at her school as a student assistant. One day, during the last period before school let out, I was to sit next to a 12-year-old girl in a science class. She was shy and quiet, with red, protruding eyes. I was to model good behavior for her (raising my hand, singing along with peers, smiling, etc.) then escort her to the little yellow bus that would take her home. Every day would end without a single response from her in class, but just as she was boarding the bus, she would take my hand and kiss it. That kiss touched my heart. I decided to become a special needs teacher.

Personal Goal Setting

I hope I have inspired you to start running, pushing yourself to the limit, and aiming for the stars.

Step into the starting blocks. Get ready to run. But first, ask yourself, what are your goals? Progress from race to race or season to season?

Let's assume that you are a newcomer to cross-country running. You go out for cross country because you have the desire. Your goal is to have fun and get in shape. You also want to improve your performance by the end of the season. You have two goals: short-term and long-term.

Setting goals takes courage. Remember, running is a solo competition, and your goals represent commitments — but only to yourself. When you share them with others, they create expectations, social pressure, and accountability.

Here is an example. All my teammates and the coach of the all-Army track team knew that my goal was to compete in the Olympic Trials, win a berth in the 1976 Olympic team and represent the United States in the

Olympics. In 1976, I represented the U.S. Army at the Pacific AAU Track and Field Championships at San Mateo College. I ran a 27:50 for six miles on the track — a meet/stadium record and the fastest ever run by a Pacific-AAU athlete, breaking Don Kardong's mark by 1.2 seconds. Kardong went on to finish fourth in the 1976 Montreal Olympics. An article in the San Francisco Chronicle the next day read: "It is going to be hard keeping Gerry out of the 1976 Olympic team." I had created expectations.

I qualified for the 1968, 1972, and 1976 Olympic Trails in the 10,000 meters, but I didn't make the team. I can't explain why I never performed well at the trials. Still, in 1982, I received a $4,000 scholarship to work on my master's in educational administration at Highland

University in Las Vegas, New Mexico. The cross-country coach there, Ron Maestas, asked me to train with his runners. I had a personal goal: I was over the hill, but I wanted to qualify for the 1984 Olympic Team in the 10,000 meters. I shared my goal with coach Maestas, and pretty soon the public relations director at Highland found out, and the next thing I knew my goal was shared by everybody at the university and in the small town. It was great! I didn't qualify to run at the trials, but I had a lot of fun.

So good luck! After you graduate from high school, you might want to continue competing in cross country. If you don't have an athletic scholarship, you can be a "walk-on." You'd be surprised how many walk-on runners receive a full scholarship every year. Remember, your goals can — and should — change, but your vision will stay the same. When an obstacle appears, do not abandon the destination, but simply adjust your course. **You can do it!**

ABOUT THE AUTHOR

I have a Master's Degrees in special education, public administration, and educational administration. I am in the doctoral program at the University of New Mexico. I taught special needs students at the Albuquerque Public Schools for more than twenty years. My last race was in 1976 at the United States Armed Forces championships at Laney College in Oakland, California. I set a new meet/stadium record in the 10,000 meters. I don't compete any more, but I still stay in shape. When I am not jogging, I like to play the guitar.

2017

www.ingramcontent.com/pod-product-compliance
Lightning Source LLC
Chambersburg PA
CBHW071309060426
42444CB00034B/1748